P9-DHO-833

Finding Your Way in the Spiritual Age

Dr. Dan Bird

© 2018 by Dr. Dan Bird

All rights reserved. No part of this book, in part or in whole, may be reproduced, transmitted or utilized in any form or by any means, electronic, photographic or mechanical, including photocopying, recording, or by any information storage and retrieval system without permission in writing from Ozark Mountain Publishing, Inc. except for brief quotations embodied in literary articles and reviews.

For permission, serialization, condensation, adaptions, or for our catalog of other publications, write to Ozark Mountain Publishing, Inc., P.O. Box 754, Huntsville, AR 72740, ATTN: Permissions Department.

Library of Congress Cataloging-in-Publication Data

Bird, Dan – 1952 -
Finding Your Way in the Spiritual Age by Dan Bird

This second book takes the newly awakened souls a step further. "Yes," they cry, "we feel there is something going on, but how does it fit into my daily life?" How do we take this new soul-level knowledge, embrace it fully, yet live in the physical world?

1. Metaphysical 2. Spiritual 3. Spirit Guides 4. Guardian Angels
I. Dan Bird, 1952 - II. Metaphysical III. Spiritual IV. Title

Library of Congress Catalog Card Number: 2018960316
ISBN: 9781940265568

Cover Art and Layout: www.vril8.com
Book set in: Lucida Sans
Book Design: Tab Pillar
Published by:

OZARK
MOUNTAIN
PUBLISHING

PO Box 754, Huntsville, AR 72740
800-935-0045 or 479-738-2348; fax 479-738-2448

WWW.OZARKMT.COM

Printed in the United States of America

For my brother, Mike, who left us far too early

For my brother, Mike, who left us far too early.

Quotes/Endorsements:

"I was lucky enough to be involved in Dan's life when his interest and passion for metaphysical learning and discussion was reemerging. To see this passion come to life in the form of his first two books is absolutely inspiring! He was born to be a teacher and has found not only a subject he is fiercely committed to, but also, his method, through writing. These books are a true gift to all who are seeking and are willing to learn."

Jodi Jorgensen, Advance copy reader

"This book is the second in a series from the author. I love how the book is helpful in lighting the path which is best for me. His book feels as though he is standing in front of a forest where there are numerous paths with different turns. He gives you the light, and the tools, to choose which path feels right and good to you. We can't all fit on the same path, we have to go the way that works for each one of us. I like that if I get lost on my way this book will guide me back to finding my path again. Dan explains finding your way in a way that it feels you are talking with one of your closest friends. You can feel he is writing from the heart and it is very reassuring and comforting while being extremely helpful all at the same time!"

Teresa Paulson, Advance copy reader

In the opening of *"Finding Your Way in the Spiritual Age"* Dr. Dan Bird says it perfectly, "This is not difficult." Dan is very relatable and his story telling abilities make his second book easy to follow. *"Finding Your Way in the Spiritual Age"* is a must read for the newly awakened to the spiritually seasoned.

Carissa Kelley
Guided By Angels, A Center For Healing

If you're new to spirituality or have been at it awhile, "*Finding Your Way in the Spiritual Age*" is a must read! Dr. Birds (Dan's) way of writing about spirituality is done in such a way that allows everyone to grasp the concepts on a very personal level! It was, like his first book, "*Waking Up in the Spiritual Age*", a real page turner that captivated us from the start! Dr. Bird (Dan) doesn't write books, per se but rather talks with someone he cares about and that is YOU!

Sandra and Alan
Twin Flame Divine Fire Radio Program
twinflamedivinefire.wixsite.com/divine-fire-
http://tfrlive.com

Dan Bird's latest book helps us with the question we all have once we experience a spiritual awakening, "Now what?" It's a resource to help us navigate our way through the detours and pitfalls while following a spiritual path. A reminder to keep an open mind and an open heart. The messages this book contains are very much needed in today's world.

Jeff Gross
Tarot Card Reader
Angels and Hawks

Contents

Contents

Preface

Once upon a time, God created the Universe, and populated it with creatures of all kinds. We, as humans, are one of those creatures and we are unique, we have free will. Free will allows us to choose how we will respond to everything around us: with anger, happiness, indifference, aggression, pure joy, sadness, and all points in between. All of these reactions are possible, and that is what makes us so interesting, and sometimes dangerous, selfless, difficult, generous, loving, or impossible. There are endless possibilities in every interaction, in fact, at every moment on Earth.

The duality of existence makes this ever more interesting, too. We are human, of flesh and blood, but we are also, and more importantly, of Spirit. We have a soul, a soul that lives forever. Our human bodies are only temporary housing for our personalities, or egos, and our souls. We learn while on Earth lessons we cannot obtain in Spirit.

This book will attempt to explain and possibly guide you in understanding the greatest desire of mankind, to know why we are here and why we exist, all told from a human perspective without esoteric jargon. In short, we are here to learn, but learn what? And how do we go about it? Is this anything like attending grammar school and onward? Not so much, this is real, this is life, the true core of why we are alive, part of everything we think and do during our lifetime on Earth. Though we are flesh and blood, with all the urges, needs, and desires that entails, we are also, at a higher level, a soul, with a whole other set of goals in mind.

Right up front I will tell you, there is no set pattern on how to live a Spiritual life; each person has their own path, with goals and experiences to encounter. It is how we respond, how we react, and what we learn from the events and relationships that teach us. Confusing? Sort of, but it gets clearer. This concept is not difficult, but our society has so clouded the truth that breaking loose from past beliefs and some ways of thinking is challenging. Humans find safety in traditional lines of thought, especially when shared with others and instilled over the course of a lifetime. Sometimes important information is left out. Information is power, and when people know they have the power they can threaten the standard belief systems. I believe some of the basic truths about the world of Spirit have been hidden from much of mankind. We are taught certain "facts" in specific ways in our churches and social groups, and most of what we are taught has been handed down from previous generations. Some things have been twisted a bit, or left out, and armed with some of this knowledge we can more easily think for ourselves, make up our own minds, and find our true Spiritual path. No one person, or group, or nation, or religion has the corner on truth. Each of us, individually, has equal power to decide, to seek, and to find the truth for ourselves. The Spiritual truth is here, and the time is now. A wonderful life of your own choosing is waiting for you if you understand how to make the connections.

Introduction

My first book, *Waking Up in the Spiritual Age*, dealt with the far-reaching changes occurring in the world today, changes at the soul level, felt deeply by so many. People all around us are asking important questions about why we are here and what our goals are in this life. By waking up I referred to those who have become aware that there is truly more to life than meets the physical senses. Becoming aware is the key; after that, questions naturally flow. No longer are the multitudes willing to simply believe what they are told to believe. Now they know they can, and must, think for themselves. This is part of the shift that has begun and is being felt at all levels, though many do not know what is happening. The shift is helping to open up the senses of those who are waking up to Spirit, but this shift is also causing fear and discomfort to those firmly entrenched in the materialistic world. The old ways are beginning to die out and a new eon is upon us, though we are witnessing its very birth at this time.

This second book takes the newly awakened souls a step further. "Yes," they cry, "we feel there is something going on, but how does it fit into my daily life?" How do we take this new soul-level knowledge, embrace it fully, yet live in the physical world? Can it work with the secular, three-dimensional world? Yes, it can, and it does. All around you are people living fully Spiritual, fulfilling, rewarding lives. Some of them do this naturally without ever realizing it. Not everyone needs this kind of book; it all depends on where you are at and what you are interested in. The answers are there for everyone, at the level they wish to understand, when they feel they are ready. There is no rush, no hurry; we have time.

If you are reading this, you are most likely interested in Spiritual matters and have taken the first steps to awaken yourself. You may simply wonder if making money, working, growing old, and dying is all there is. You think, maybe what we were taught in church is worth revisiting, and even feels right, though maybe it doesn't feel quite right. So, you look a little further and run into the ever-growing information in books, videos, magazines, movies, and television programs asking, and sometimes answering, the same questions you have. Hmmm, so what's next? If the ideas presented in this book and others "resonate" with you, that is, you recognize some truth at a deep level, then you are ready to move on, to discover the richness of living in Spirit each day. Read on and you'll find what has worked for me and changed my life. Looking at the world with an understanding of Spirit changes your perception. You no longer are ruled by the suggestions of ego that everything is bad or could be bad! No, you see beyond it, you see the shining center of the image, the situation, the person. This is what waking up and living a Spiritual life is all about. It is the way we were meant to live; positive, loving, and compassionate.

In *Waking Up in the Spiritual Age* I wrote about my own childhood, how I grew up without attending church while very young, so missed the indoctrination period many went through; that is, up until age nine when my family moved and I was then placed in a religious school and told what to think, how to pray, and especially what sin was! Repent! Feel bad! Be sorry! Don't sin anymore! Repent! But first you have to tell someone (priest) what you did wrong. Well, did I use bad words five times? No, I didn't really curse as a child. So, what did I confess? Impure thoughts was a good one, right? I didn't know what they were but we heard about them in religion class. I didn't know what to tell him, so I usually made some stuff up. I was mean to my sister two times, I yelled at someone three times, and on and on. OK, say three Hail Marys and one Our Father. Off you go. Yay, now my soul was clean as the fresh snow! I apologize if I seem a bit snarky here. I mean no disrespect. The traditional forms of religion work well for many people.

But as I grew a little older I started questioning things. Why did that priest have the power to forgive sins I committed? Did God talk to him? How was he chosen? Why couldn't I talk to God myself? I really didn't understand the go-between that I was told was necessary. I think the years of no church (we lived in a very small town without a Catholic church, and my mom was raised Catholic) caused me to think just a bit differently. I just couldn't buy into everything blindly, but I found out you are expected to accept the teachings without question, "Because we say so." I tried my best to believe and accept, but failed. Nothing against the church; it just didn't work well for me. This led me onto my own Spiritual path. I found a few books that asked those questions, and they just felt right. The next thing I knew, I had met many like-minded people who felt the same. It continues to grow to this day, and this book is for those who are looking to grow with us.

Chapter 1

What Is a Spiritual Life?

The question here is whether you want to lead a Spiritual life while on Earth. What does that mean? If a life is "Spiritual," is it not the physical life I'm leading? Are they different? Can they exist at the same time? Do I have to die first to be Spiritual? Is a Spiritual life better than a physical life? These are where we start. Questions lead to thought and inspiration, and possibly intuition, which can result in answers.

The duality of physical (of the Earth) and Spiritual existence is difficult to grasp in our human world. We know that we have a body, and we are told we have a soul, as well. Together they make up who we are, but we can't see the soul, can we? The soul is the everlasting, most important part of who we are, and we are actually here in the physical form to provide opportunities for our soul to learn and grow.

The Spiritual world is located here, where we are. We can't see it due to the vibrational speed in which we operate. We are too low in frequency (most of the time) to tap into the next level. The Earth is probably on the lowest level of the many leading to God or Source, but it is important because so much can be experienced and learned here. The next dimension vibrates much faster, and communication between the two is not always easy. Some people have a natural talent for raising their vibrations and connecting in various ways with the next realm. Psychics, mediums, and others who have developed this ability may be able to connect with those who have passed on to the Spirit world. But the truth is, we all have these abilities and use them, though we are not always aware of it. Have you ever had a hunch about something? Or maybe you decided to drive a different way home from work one evening, only to find out later there was a huge accident on your regular route? There are many ways we connect, learn from, and communicate with the nonphysical entities who watch over us.

The question remains: *but how can I best live in this Spiritual age?* It is actually quite simple, but you have to be at the point in your life and development that it is within your true self. If you are waking up to the world of Spirit, you are on your way and are taking the first steps. Many have not felt the stirrings of Spirit yet, and this book may not resonate with them. If it feels right to you, you are ready to move forward. Living a Spiritual life is an attitude, a philosophy, but mostly it is the way you interpret your life and your relationships to those around you. It is within you and affects you in every aspect of your existence. This is not a temporary focus, if you truly feel it, expect it to last a lifetime. Living it is simple, and hopefully the "how" will be made clearer in the following chapters.

What Living a Spiritual Life Is Not

It might be a good idea to dispel of some of the incorrect notions we find in the public. Living a life of Spirit is not walking around with a "holy" attitude all day, or wearing saffron robes, or repeating your mantra by the hour, or walking on hot coals, or going to church, or smelling of incense, though you certainly can do any and all of those if you want to. Nothing wrong with any approach, but they are not *requirements*, and if anyone tells you they are, they are mistaken. A Spiritual life is within you, the outer signs are just that, signs. Spirit is inside, at a higher level than you can express. The truly Spiritual person needs not to show it, or talk about it, or bring attention to it, but rather they will live it. In their daily actions, words, and thoughts they are guided by Spirit. Perhaps you know someone who seems content, well balanced, rarely upset, who treats others well, no matter who they are or what they do. They go about their business and even seem to draw people to themselves without trying. Others sense they are to be trusted, and seek advice, or just to spend time with them. This is important when you look at the old rule of "like attracts like" in the world of Spirit and energy. You may be this way yourself, and if so, wonderful, you are moving in the right direction!

One example of a Spiritual man was Jesus. He was a modest man who did not make a fuss about himself. He led by example, and spoke of the Spiritual way, but many of his words have been reinterpreted by our religions, though that is another story. Looking at the Spiritual aspects of his life, he said that each of us can do what he could do, and better! He was pointing out that leading a Spiritual life could be accomplished by all. Yes, he was a son of God, but each and every one of us is also a son or daughter of God! Jesus wanted to show us how to live our lives in the most useful, fruitful way. Revisiting Jesus's words with a Spiritual viewpoint changes their meaning. Suddenly we see that he was not talking about sin and punishment, but rather about love and Spirit. He was a gentle man and wanted to explain that Heaven and God were within us. His words were interpreted and changed by the church to try to convince us that we must work through the church and priests to find our true God. This becomes about power, and the only real power comes from within, not from a church.

Many people belong to established churches and are happy with their choice, and that is fine. One of the reasons churches are popular is because they "explain" God to you; they lay out the rules, how to pray, and translate the words of Jesus and the Bible so you can understand. What if I told you that you don't need the church or even the Bible to be Spiritually fulfilled? I said "need," meaning you can do it yourself. If you feel the church is right for you that is great, but for some it won't answer all the questions they have. This was the case for me. Many, like me, have questions that can't be answered in a way that makes sense. If you have begun the Spiritual awakening process, you may find you aren't feeling the same, that you have a bigger picture in mind now. You can certainly continue with the church you are comfortable with, and some are very Spiritual, but again, some are not so much. I truly believe God is within each of us equally; no one has a stronger bond with God because they say so. All are God's children.

Religion and Spirituality

There is much confusion about these two words, religion and Spirituality; are they the same thing? Many think they are. If I go to church faithfully every Sunday (or Saturday or Wednesday, whichever day it is), then I am a Spiritual person, right? Possibly, but attending church is not the key to being Spiritual. It is the going within via meditation or other means that allow for it. The act of going to church or anywhere is simply an action, and though Spirituality can lead our actions, true Spirit comes from within, in the heart, and is developed by your own interest and desire. You absolutely can go to church and be Spiritual, but it is not the act of going that does it, though being with a group of people praying and taking part in religious rituals can be very positive!

Religion, in my view, is a coordinated, organized way of connecting with God, with leaders who help us, and this can be very useful, but if they ask you to reach God through them, I have to disagree. No one has a more direct connection than we do, all of us. God is within us and there is no real need for a middleman, so to speak. Unfortunately, some religions become caught up in the power of leadership, of having people answer to them, and money. Look out for the constant request for money; it shows that there is a material side of the church that can get out of control. Bigger buildings, more flash, TV programs, and mega-churches can become cults of personality with pastors who start out maybe with positive motives, but slip up due to the desire for power and money. We've seen the fall of many so-called false prophets in our own time, and there will be more. Unfortunately, some people allow for others to tell them about God, to be their connection, and worse, tell them what God has told them directly. They have no more connection to God than you do. It is sad how gullible some folks are, and they will often be let down in a matter of time. True connection to God comes within each of us, individually, not through a pastor, priest, or guru. They can help lead us, but it is up to us to make the real connections.

Living in Spirit

Writing about, talking about, reading about, or listening about Spirit is not the same as living it. Those are all worthy activities, but they all pale in comparison to living it fully. This is my second book on this topic, but I am no expert. I am merely forwarding information along to those interested of what I've found through meditation, contemplation, and, yes, trying to live it. I fail often, but I learn in my failings. This is important. You can't suddenly decide to be a Spiritual person and BANG!—there you are! Holy! Enlightened! Not exactly, though there have been some in history who claim this is true. I believe we are all here to learn, to love, to experience life, and to find our true path back to Source, or God. The path of Spirit is often a slow, one-step-at-a-time kind of path, with bumps along the way, but don't despair! If you are drawn into these ideas, you have already started! If you haven't or know of others who haven't begun consciously on their path, that is OK.

Each and every one of us has our own goals, no two lives are identical, so remember to never judge another. Probably even more important: don't judge yourself! No matter what you have done. Move on. When we judge we are using our own point of reference, a point of reference that has no value whatsoever for others! It is a blind point of reference that has no way of fairly judging anyone, including ourselves. Sounds harsh, but when you understand this you back off from judgment, which is a big step in the right direction. Just becoming aware that we are doing this is a moving forward.

A Little Background

It feels like time for me to back up a bit, and for anyone reading this book who has not read *Waking Up in the Spiritual Age*, a little background. In the introduction to this book I mentioned growing up without formal religious training until I was about nine years of age. I still feel this was part of the reason I began searching for more information about why we are here and where we will ultimately go. Having a questioning mind really helps. The "Because I say so!" line just doesn't work for me; I need more. My search was solitary for most of my life.

I didn't know of others who were interested in this topic. I only had books I found until a few years ago when a friend told me of a group of people who met regularly to discuss Spiritual topics. She invited me to attend a meeting, and that did it! It started my new awakening. I found that other people did think about these things, and they talked about them and shared their thoughts, feelings, and experiences! When I walked out of that meeting, I truly felt I was walking on air. I found out later that these discussions, when from the heart, lift the vibrational levels of everyone present. And it is real. I didn't want to leave! I went back for more meetings and was introduced to many wonderful people, some who had amazing talents: mediums, those who communicate directly with the departed; psychics who can foresee possible future events in various ways; Reiki energy practitioners, but there were also many, if not most, who haven't felt strong esoteric skills, yet sensed they were real. Maybe they had witnessed unusual occurrences that they just didn't feel were coincidences.

The important point is that we were all drawn together. We felt like outcasts in a sense, we were not of the mainstream in our beliefs, and we were no longer alone. There was something happening here that was important. Don't get me wrong; as in all things, eventually we had visitors at our meetings who wanted to challenge our concepts or always wanted proof of this or that. I am thankful for them, because they showed me that everyone is at a different place in their path. Many of those guests eventually stopped attending; they were not getting the attention they wanted anymore. But the group of wonderful people that I met allowed me to begin thinking out loud, experiencing new ideas and ways to approach my life, and it felt like I was finally home. Let me add to this that as time goes on you may or may not feel the desire to attend these meetings; you will change and grow. Suddenly you realize your path has veered a bit, and you wish to explore Spirituality on your own for a while. You may also feel strongly that continuing to attend is just what you need. Don't force it, don't attend if you don't feel the need. Within each of us are the true answers.

I began to keep a Spiritual journal. It grew very rapidly, and after a while I started sending occasional entries to some like-minded friends. Their feedback was positive and I began to think that the information was coming to me (through me?) at such a rapid pace that maybe I should write a book. I felt very passionate about the material, and it was not difficult to work out the details and write the chapters. At this point I decided I would send out a cover letter, a couple of chapters, and the other requested materials to publishers. I was lucky enough, after a few rejections, to land on the desks at Ozark Mountain Publishers, LLC. I was asked to send the rest of the manuscript to them, and subsequently they decided to publish the book. Here is the interesting part of this story: after my first rejections I was feeling that maybe I was misreading the signs, and I wasn't to write books at all. So, I put the whole thing out of my head (sort of) and offered it to the Universe. I basically said, "If this book is to be published I offer it to you!" It wasn't long after that that I heard from Ozark. The universe will provide you with what you need on your path, and this has been shown to me many times. You can substitute God or Source or Spirit for Universe in this. Ask and you will receive.

Chapter 2

Why Are We Here?

Become a people watcher of sorts, see how individuals behave and react to the various happenings of the day. After a while you may see patterns, and maybe you can begin to predict how someone will respond to certain stimuli. OK, enough of those "other" people; how about watching yourself? This can become very interesting. Honest observation of your actions and reactions, your first thoughts, as well as follow-up thoughts, and how you reason through situations can be very enlightening; that is, if you are brave enough to really look at what is happening. We, as humans, sometimes skirt around the truth, and kind of bend what we observe to fit our own preconceptions. If you can be honest you can learn so much more.

But, what does this have to do with why we are here? It is tied in, make no mistake about it. We were born as humans on this planet it is true, with much forethought and planning, and with many challenges as well as joys to experience. Lots of ups and downs, successes and failures, happiness and sadness, and everything in between. Experience. Feel. Know. Live. Love. Be who we are, and see where that takes us. Some will bravely go where their heart and soul takes them, some might not be as outgoing, and find a less active way to live their lives. Both are 100 percent approved! Each and every life is meant to be lived in the way the individual chooses. No one else has any say at all. Can you believe it? Only you get to decide what you want your life to look like.

Being here on Earth allows us to have adventures one might say, adventures in many locations, with an assortment of people, or on our own. So much is available. This is where we come back to observing ourselves. Within each of these adventures we are going to find out that we are multifaceted individuals. We can't fully predict how we'll react. But with each new situation, by careful self-observation, and a strong core belief in who we are, we can more often than not make the right decisions for our own Spiritual growth. And that is the key to why we are here, for our Spiritual enlightenment and growth. There is much that can be felt and experienced on Earth that is simply not available in the other realms. There is a desire in many Spiritual beings to enter the physical world, to feel and understand the emotions and sensations available to us on Earth. This is a new concept, that someone would wish to leave "Heaven" and come to the three-dimensional world. The speed of growth is much higher, and the rewards greater, though at the cost of a life sometimes filled with sorrow, pain, and turmoil. But many lives are filled with joy and happiness, too. Most have plenty of everything and are so valuable!

Some believe that the earthly plane is the lowest, densest level of existence, and once we move on from here we reach higher, lighter levels until we return to our natural home in Source, or God. Earth is the place to start, to really feel, to learn. We are learning all the time at the Spiritual level, even though we are mostly unaware of it. Our true selves, our souls, are always alert, but our human side, our egos or personalities, don't automatically know this. When we start wondering if there is more to life, and if there is a real reason to exist, we have begun the process of Spiritual awakening, of learning what we have "forgotten" when we came to Earth.

Plans and Blueprints

Before we were born we put together a plan of sorts with our Spirit Guides for this lifetime. We examined what we needed to work on, what situations would allow for the most growth, what our karma demanded of us, and how we could be of best use for others we would interact with. Souls often incarnate together over many lifetimes, though in changing earthly roles. It is possible to be someone's father in one incarnation only to return as their child in the next, or as a friend. There are countless possible connections. Of course, over the many lifetimes we may live there will be some in which certain entities are not involved. But we have a road map of who we will be related to, who we will work closely with, who we will marry, and even who our children will be. These are worked out before we incarnate.

Have you ever wondered why you can meet someone new and instantly like them? Or strongly dislike them? What draws us to some and away from others? This goes beyond simple looks. There are connections at a deeper level, remembrances from previous lives together in which there were problems. How strange would it be if you were a doctor operating to save a man's life, a man who murdered you in a previous life? Or possibly you killed him before and are doing your best to save him this go round. You may have a uncharacteristic desire to do all you can to save him, even beyond the usual level of caring you bring to work with you. On the surface you don't understand why this is so very important to you; after all, you don't even know this man, right? But at the soul level you do, you know him very well. You may have shared multiple lives together.

A wonderful psychic told me that my wife and I had been together in many lifetimes and were actually a couple in Paris a few hundred years ago. In that lifetime, however, I was the female and she the male. I will admit that this was a strange thought for me, and it took a while to get my hands around it. We can identify so strongly with our current gender that we find it difficult to understand that we have been both in the past. This is part of the male/female energy balance we hear about. As souls we are both genders or more likely, neither, and it is important to experience both when we incarnate.

The plans we make before birth are general outlines of what will occur during that life. Included will be a number of other people who agreed to be a part of our lives, and we agreed to be part of theirs. Those you feel strongly attached to are probably of your soul group. You have revolving roles to be sure, but still your energies identify with each other and you will be important parts of each other's lives. Imagine what life would be like if we knew those connections in our lives; if we knew how we were together in the past? Amazing. Some psychics are talented at looking at our past lives and can give you some strong hints and connect some dots for you if you are interested. The records of our past lives are available to us.

If someone does something that upsets you or is cruel, even horrible to you, you can look at it this way: how would your attitude toward them change if you knew they had planned out that behavior *with you* before you came to this planet? You needed to learn a lesson of some kind and needed that treatment to learn it. Another soul agreed to play the role, and even if it was distasteful or harmful, it was to help you with your karma. This changes our whole mindset, doesn't it?

Part of waking up Spiritually is to recognize this in others, to see that we cannot judge a book by its cover! Each person is a soul, the same as we are, and they are playing various roles to help them and us to grow and learn on a Spiritual level. A person may have agreed to have a terrible disease, not because they needed it for their karma, but to help their caretakers with theirs! Is there a greater love than this?

Returning to the Physical World

No lifetime on Earth is wasted, all are valuable to our Spiritual growth. Each and every person you see is on the same journey, to learn, to experience, and to feel. These lessons are available in their fullest on this dimensional plane. It is so easy to forget this, to view others in less than positive ways, to forget they have their own goals and reasons for being here. We must not only accept that, we must celebrate it! We must also celebrate our own existence! Each and every day we can look around and see the beauty of life, the opportunities to feel and freely think, to see there is so much more than our often narrow focus tells us. Becoming aware of the vastness of life, of the physical as well as the Spiritual worlds, leads us to much higher levels of thinking and living, and our lessons become part of our everyday life. No lesson is wasted, but continues to add to our experience while here, always enriching and enlightening us as we learn.

The reasons that souls decide to return to Earth are many. Lessons that haven't been covered to the extent deemed necessary, to repay karma, to balance debts of past lives, and many more. Souls are anxious to return, ready to deal with all kinds of situations, including poverty, disease, difficulties of all sorts, and even serious physical problems. It's even possible you decided on a life of riches and luxury, and the test for you may be how you decide to use those riches. Each soul is equal in the sight of God, and those lessons, though selected specifically for that lifetime, are valuable and important to that soul. If we remember this when dealing with others it changes our attitude. We now realize that the circumstances each individual finds themselves in were chosen for growth. The conscious mind may not recognize this, but the soul-level subconscious does, and as we awaken Spiritually we see it, too.

An amazing thing happens: we see the similarities in others rather than the differences as we grow in Spirit. There is much less of "them" and "us" now; it is only all of us, in this together, and we can choose to help one another along. Not everyone is awake yet, so walking up to a stranger and telling them that we are Spiritual brothers and sisters may not be a very good idea at this time. Best to simply treat others as if they were our actual brothers and sisters, accepting that we are one together as a family and are meant to help one another along in this incarnation. I am really referring to the small things, such as saying "Hello!" when happening upon someone during a walk. Simple politeness, recognizing there is a person here, that they matter, that they count, can make a difference in that person's life. Small steps can yield big results. Sometimes the smallest action can affect another in ways we wouldn't even think possible. I believe we should always try to be kind and polite to everyone, recognizing that their value and path is theirs alone, but runs alongside of ours.

We are here to learn. This is accomplished in many ways, through interactions with others, as well as on our own. Living in a Spiritual age such as this is a wonderful opportunity to move forward, ever closer to Source, where we came from. Every day we have opportunities to learn and to share what we learn, often through our own actions and reactions. As we grow in Spirit we more often choose the right path for growth and to help others. Again, these choices can be very small, like holding a door for someone with their arms loaded down or allowing another car in line ahead of you. Simple. Observe and act, and if you choose to be kind and friendly the world we live in wins, even in small ways.

We are here to experience. This includes sadness, pain, happiness, euphoria, and all things in between. No one has a completely happy life, as no one has a lifetime devoid of sadness and challenge. We all live lives that provide every feeling imaginable. Some lives were planned with great, terrible challenges, and some with less difficulty, but they were chosen for the lessons needed. So, do we then just allow those who are suffering to simply "learn their lessons" and not try to help? NO! This would be a terrible mistake. What if a person in your family chose in their life plan to suffer a terrible physical trauma or disease? Is it their problem? Yes and no. Think about this: what if they volunteered to suffer to help YOU with a karmic debt? What level of love is that? The highest! This goes for anyone suffering. We don't know why pain chose them rather than us, but be aware we may well be involved. How do we choose to respond? With compassion and love? Or with avoidance and fear? This lifetime might have been created just for this lesson. If we fail it, well, no worries, we will return for another in the future to try to learn the lesson again. Why not now? Now is always a good time because now is all we really have.

Chapter 3

Waking Up

Just what is this waking up to Spirit and how does it feel? Great questions; unfortunately, there are one hundred answers for every one hundred people going through this process. In general, inside you will feel drawn to something that catches your attention and sort of opens the door just a bit. Many have felt something inside for a long time, but the door hadn't really opened for them yet. They knew something was missing from their lives, something unnamed. Some try to fill that gap with more money or buying more "stuff" or building power or in drugs or alcohol. There are many ways to try to feel more complete. They don't work, however. More is never enough. This is because the lack they feel is within, and until they see the connections to Spirit they will continue to miss the boat (even if they buy more boats).

Using my own life as an example, I felt drawn to the Spiritual ways as a teenager, but didn't have any idea what it was or how to get there. My own life felt empty in some ways. I somehow found myself with a book of Spirituality, *Your Mysterious Powers of ESP* by Harold Sherman, published in 1969. I have no idea to this day where this book came from, or how it fell into my hands, but it introduced me to many beautiful concepts that I knew intuitively were right, at least for me. I learned about telepathy, communicating with those who have passed, Spiritual healing, and much more; and despite the title, it is a very positive and energizing book.

I still have the book and return to it occasionally to remember my first time with these ideas. I had no one else to discuss these life-changing topics with so I continued to study and buy new books as I found them on my own. There was something so real here I knew I would never return to my old ways of thinking.

Many years later I was introduced to a Spiritual group that met monthly. I attended on the recommendation of a friend, and I found exactly what I had been missing. There were others who felt this way! Others who studied and talked about, and best of all, lived in a more Spiritual way! I walked out of that meeting floating on air. I had found a sort of home base, and wasn't alone. Interestingly enough most of those in attendance had felt the same way at one time until discovering this and other groups.

So I attended the meetings and found many interesting individuals who had the ability to do psychic readings or who were mediums able to connect with our dead loved ones. The more events and discussions I attended, the more I felt this was right. Yet, this good feeling did not come without some trepidation. After the first glow wore off a bit, I noticed there were some who attended who wanted to "top" the others; in other words, some wanted to show the group they were more advanced or more developed in a Spiritual way. Sometimes two would go back and forth trying to be more knowledgeable or experienced. Their egos wanted attention. Interestingly enough, those kinds of individuals usually didn't come to many meetings before they wore out their welcome. No one said anything, but the others stopped giving them energy and they stopped coming. Even in the world of Spirituality there are egos hard at work. The temptation to feel "special" when Spiritual gifts are discovered is strong, and it is wonderful to find that some talented folks can stay above ego's demands, but some can't.

I felt I was truly awakening to a new world, and it felt right. I wanted more interactions with like-minded folks, those who were opening up to Spirit in the same way, so I, along with my wife, Kathie, invited two friends over for Spiritual discussions at our house. They had been attending the sessions along with us and also felt some of the competition in the meetings. This small group began weekly meetings, very informal, but very valuable. We were able to help each other understand these topics and to grow Spiritually. The discussions were such a success that a few others found out about them and asked if they could attend. We expanded the group to about eight, but wanted to keep it small. A group was formed, and we've become very close and supportive! The group continues to this day, though we may not meet weekly, sometimes it is monthly, depending on work schedules and so on, of course. We are in communication via phone, e-mail, and text messages regularly. Finding, or forming, a supportive group like this directly led me to write this book as well as the first one, *Waking Up in the Spiritual Age.* I had never planned on writing a book, but after sharing some journal writing with the group dealing with my Spiritual changes they suggested I write a book, so there you go. You just never know, do you? All of this, which continues, came about from the waking up we have all gone through.

What's Next?

As each of us wakes up to the world of Spirit, and it begins to feel right, we naturally ask ourselves "what is next?" In other words, what should I do now? We are just not sure. Do you have to meditate, pray, or offer thanks all the time? No, but they can sure help to move the Spiritual energy along. Meditation allows for the quieting of the busy mind and is an opportunity for the soul, or higher self, to communicate with you. This is often, if not always, pretty subtle, and works with your subconscious, but you will be provided with guidance and support. The next major decision you may need to make could be easier for you, you will just "know" what to do. This can come from Spiritual guidance and may be enhanced by meditation.

Keep in mind that all the group discussions and books, videos, etc., only help you so far, the real growth occurs within. No one else can do it for you; they can only help with suggestions and techniques for meditating and offering support. The important Spiritual advancements are made individually. Meditation helps you find the answers.

What is meditation? Quiet time, non-thinking time. Usually thought of as sitting quietly in an inviting, calm environment for a spell, it can also be working on the yard, playing music, and more; there are many healthy ways to quiet the mind without drugs or alcohol. That quiet time when we sort of shut off the physical mind is important.

How Quickly Do We Wake Up?

Some feel they have been Spiritually awake their entire lives, and they felt and knew things as small children. They may not have known quite what was going on, but they dealt with it the best they could. And the best way in our society has often been to hide what is happening. Children were often not encouraged to discuss the Spiritual beings they could sense and sometimes talk with. These children, who could feel others' emotions (empathy), were often made to feel that was not "normal" and they would choose to hide it. Sometimes that worked, but often it faded for a time only to return when a bit older. Then there are those who were encouraged and found open-minded people around them, often their parents. They were the lucky ones. But each path in life is valuable, though some have rockier trails to walk.

Many of us have had our share of psychic or Spiritual happenings throughout our lives, many of which we dismissed, or tried to forget, or mostly believed they were coincidences. Often we simply didn't have the knowledge to recognize what was happening. Why was a certain old song coming on the radio, and then in a movie, and on TV? We easily could miss the connection with our favorite cousin who passed away last year. There are many ways to communicate from the Spiritual realm, but they are often very subtle and can be missed if we are not looking for them or are not tuned in, so to speak.

The process of waking up can also be instantaneous according to some, but I don't know of anyone personally who felt they became fully awake that way. In almost all cases it is a gradual development and may take a lifetime. I believe waking up to Spirit is a process, not an event. We begin with our first awareness. Something is happening, something more is going on that I am sort of sensing, but I'm not sure. Then a little information comes along, or I have a dream that feels very real in which I start to question things. There are many simple steps that move us forward on our path. So why do we want to wake up Spiritually at all? Can we go through life without it? After all, we set up a life plan before we incarnated on Earth and agreed to come here without memory of our Spiritual self, right? So why would we want some of that lost knowledge? Well, we could do just fine without it, but with the information of who we really are and why we are here we can reshape our lives in a much more fulfilling way. We have clues that move us along. We view our time on Earth in a completely new way, since we now know it is temporary and we will be reunited with our passed loved ones in a matter of time. We are to experience life to the fullest! Waking up helps with that understanding. We wouldn't accomplish as much or grow the same way if we came to Earth with full knowledge of where we are from. We need the lessons of the physical world to help us grow.

Signs You Are Waking Up

When we begin to wake up to Spirit we may notice things a little differently. Our senses may become more alive. The sky is bluer, the breeze is fresher, smells are stronger. Is this real or simply our imagination? I think we notice things more clearly. It certainly has been that way for my wife, Kathie, and myself. When we walk the dogs, we notice so much more than we used to notice, such as the rays coming through the clouds at dawn, the slight changing of the leaves as autumn moves in, or the sound of different trees as their leaves blow in the wind. Yes, everyone can see and hear these things, and probably do; the difference that I've seen is that we are more aware of them, and slow down to take note of them, to share what we are seeing and hearing and feeling. Waking up is subtle, but it is real, and slowing down our ever-increasing pace of living helps a great deal.

There are signs all around, but we often just don't notice them. For me, finding pennies (and feathers) is always a positive jolt. When I find these, my thoughts turn to my family and friends who have passed or even to my Spirit Guides who may want to say hello. Being aware and rather than see everything that happens as a coincidence, try to accept what happens and gently examine to see if there is a connection. You may have a sudden thought about someone or something that is triggered by a "coincidence," and it may bring a thought to you or an emotion. Don't force an interpretation on the incident, but accept it and allow it to be. After a while you may notice more of these things happening, and you will learn, or more likely feel, if there is indeed a connection or message for you.

As I wrote earlier, a key to moving into a Spiritual life is to find ways to quiet the ever-moving mind. Meditation is the well-known way to do this, but it is not the only way. For many it is a wonderful exercise to shut off the noise running through your head incessantly. Just try to sit down for five minutes and ask your brain to take a break! Not so easy, usually. Thoughts just keep flying and running along like a ticker tape or scroll on a computer screen. Frustrating when you are trying to empty the mind, isn't it? This happens to most people, and it takes a while to get the mind to behave. Meditation may take some time to really get a handle on, but it is worth it. Even two minutes of shutting down is valuable. Why? Because that is when the soul, or your higher self, connects with who you really are, and with God or Source. It seems like nothing's happening, but it is the opposite; there is communication at a very high level that you, as a human, are not aware of, though sometimes glimpses will come through to your conscious mind. These are intuitions and hunches that are very important in the waking up of Spirit. Now, understand that intuitions and hunches and feelings can happen at any time, awake, asleep, working, driving, you do not have to be meditating, but sometimes the connection from meditation opens the channels and really helps. When you feel a sign or message is for you, don't intellectualize it, instead internalize it, make it a part of you, accept it as if it were a breath of air, natural as can be, and future signs from loved ones and guides will be easier to notice. Be careful to not overreact. Let's say you get a feeling and decide to just go with it. OK, but what if the feeling you have is that you need to go punch your coworker in the nose? Sometimes the ego pushes a "feeling" on you that is negative. Be aware of that and you'll know it's not a good idea to punch them, right? Right!

In the paragraph above I said meditation is not the only way. There are actually many ways to connect with Spirit. Anything that focuses your mind will work. Playing or listening to music, painting, just about anything, even work! Quieting the mind is the important part. Going for a walk and noticing the world around you, ignoring the daily human worries and stress for a bit can be very beneficial. Listening to the rain on a summer afternoon, to the surf on a beach, or to the sounds of night in the woods, even the sound of your tires as you drive, can all quiet your mind.

When you learn to quiet the mind a bit you find yourself in alignment with the Spiritual path you are on this time around on Earth. That path has many opportunities for Spiritual growth lined up for you that were decided before you were born! You will decide how you want to deal with them, how to react, and what you will ultimately learn from them.

Chapter 4

Held Up by Past Thinking Patterns

A central theme in the world of Spiritual thought is the concept of time: that it does not exist. Wow, that's pretty intense, and very difficult to understand. So how about a little simpler way of looking at it? Our past is gone, never to return. Our future is not here, and never will be. Why? Because as soon as it seems to come along it becomes the present. And that is the important part of this, that we have *only the now.* Only this very moment that you are reading these words. That is real, nothing else is, only this very moment. Our lives are series of moments, but the only real moment is now. By being aware that the present moment is the only real thing, we are able to focus in a more useful way.

Yes, you have a past, but as I said, it is gone, and you really can't go back. So what are all these memories, you say? They happened, it is true, and they served their purpose, to help you grow and understand. Some events of the past don't seem to have any value, but they do. This is often not known for a long time, if ever, but at the soul level everything that happens is valuable, both the good and the bad. It is important to realize that your memories of the past are valid, they are real, but the events are gone, not here anymore. You live in the now only. So use the memories and past to look back on for inspiration and to learn from, just don't live in those memories. We all know someone, might be you, who often thinks about and talks about some era in their life, maybe high school, or college, or some other time. It is possible to get so caught up in those times that it becomes very difficult to move past them. This is where an understanding of living in the present moment is helpful. This instant is the key to it all, and if you look at it honestly, it is the only time you have, right now! Confusing? Yes, but let it sit there and think about it, it will clear up.

This chapter's title, *Held Up by Past Thinking Patterns*, is really not enough. Being caught up in the past does not allow for growth of the individual. This also applies to the future. Of course, you can't be stuck in the future; it isn't here, and never will be; everything becomes the present. If you spend a great deal of time thinking about the future, planning for the future, and postponing your life, so to speak, for the wonderful future you have planned, you are missing the most important part of life, right now! It is perfectly all right to make plans of various kinds for the future, but to dwell on them to the point of ignoring the richness of your life at this moment would cause you to miss out. Always remind yourself that all you really have is now, and this is the moment to think about and be in tune with. For instance, if you find yourself worrying about how your uncle in New York is doing, and you are very concerned, yet there is nothing you can do, wouldn't it be better to not worry, maybe say a prayer and send some positive thoughts and energy his way instead? Worry is a form of fear, and fear is the biggest obstacle to growth in pretty much every endeavor on Earth. Fear in its many forms brings energy down and pushes you outside not only your comfort zone, but also outside your sensible thoughts. Fear has many forms, including as I mentioned, worry, as well as anxiety, anger, and negative thoughts. We must try our best to rise above worry and fear; it is a crippling emotion.

Changing Energy

As I was meditating recently a thought kept occurring in my mind about the craziness in the world lately. Do you ever wonder why some things seem so out of whack, why there appears to be a great deal of anger and frustration? Are you sometimes caught up in this energy? Certainly we are bombarded by TV, radio, social media, texts, and so on. The news seems to mostly be bad, and each day it gets a little worse. So is this how it really is? Or are we being manipulated and played by those in power? Big questions! I think it is a bit of both. Certainly, fear is a major driving force in the world at this time, and unfortunately many do buy into it. But take a look at yourself and your own situation. Of course, there may be challenges, there may be heartbreaks, there may be situations that seem hopeless at times, but do you have a roof over your head, food, clothing, and a little spending money? Are you in reasonable health? I'm saying that there are always those nagging issues that have the power to keep us down, depressed, and worried, if we let them. If you balance out the goods and bads in your life, you will be surprised how good things are, most of the time.

That being said, yes, the news is full of disasters and murders, and so on, and as it is often said of the news: "If it bleeds, it leads!" And that is how it goes. What would happen if you refused to watch the news? What if you didn't read the paper or listen to talk radio? Would your life change? Would it frighten you to miss out on the daily happenings? Or would you simply learn to focus on your surroundings, your personal life, your own thoughts? An interesting experiment worth thinking about. Maybe some kinds of ignorance can be bliss.

A possible explanation came to me during meditation that wouldn't let go and I added it to this book immediately. I've thought about this for some time, but it was simply an idea until I picked it up in my quiet time. It goes something like this: we are entering the first stages of the so-called Age of Aquarius, a time foretold to be a positive, joyful, happy time in the history of our world. If you watch the world events you wonder if this can even be possible. So what is happening is a slow but steady raising of the vibrational rate of the earth, and everyone feels it. How each person reacts is of great interest. It won't stop, and there are many more waking up to Spirit all the time. It's tuning into the higher vibrations that are triggering this waking up. Many will learn to move with it, and find themselves within, and will flourish, while others will be uncomfortable. This will lead to a division among people, and it will confuse many. If you are awakening Spiritually you will understand; if not, it may be more of a challenge, but we will all get through it one way or another. Those who are not comfortable with the change may choose to fight it tooth and nail. They may argue and try anything to hold on to their power, riches, old grudges, anger, and so on. They will continue to feel things slipping away, the old ways they feel safe in are changing, and they simply don't know why or how. In fact, they probably don't care, and they just want to do whatever is necessary to stop the flow of change. This shows they are more comfortable at a lower vibrational rate and the increasing rate is confusing them. The higher the rate, the more positive the energy. It is what we really need, but many will fight it. You can see this clearly in our own government today, and indeed, the world shows a great deal of difficulty with this changing of the guard, so to speak. We will have to ride out this wave of division, and this is why so many are awakening at this time, to smooth over the difficulties with the transition. In fact, many Spiritually gifted babies are coming into the world at this time and will help the coming generations with the changes.

Masculine and Feminine Energy

So, why all the fear? Well, for a long time we've been under a masculine energy. So much so that we have gotten out of balance. War, aggression, power, money, while not necessarily limited to males, at this time in history seem to be more common in males, and we are often taught to be this way, to "be a man" to "show them who's boss!" Never show fear, in fact never show any emotion, because it shows you are weak! This is the masculine energy dominating. But I will tell you something, the happiest human beings are those who have balanced their male/female energies. That is a huge statement! They have *balanced* the male *and* female energies within themselves. It doesn't mean you are not masculine or feminine; it means you are balanced. You can understand the opposite gender better, you care about what they are feeling; you care about what all people are feeling. Being in balance with the divine energies, both masculine and feminine, puts you where you should be, and certainly is Spiritually positive. Balance of the energies in both males and females is the goal. Again, this does not mean you, as a man, now act less "manly" or as a woman are less "feminine." Instead, you see the bigger picture, and the difficulties between the sexes in our time are a personal issue for you. Everyone is at their own place in this, and there is no right or wrong, but it is useful to understand the changes occurring.

We've been in a male energy period for a long time, and the shift that has started will help bring us into a much better balance, maybe even a "golden age" of humanity. This may take a while to get there, but it will be wonderful.

If you believe in reincarnation, as I do, and you know you've been both male and female in past lives, it makes sense that a balance would be needed as you move forward. As souls we are both genders, or maybe neither; we are simply energy, balanced energy. So it makes sense that whichever sex we are, we should align ourselves with the opposite side, and understand each other so that we can all move forward together.

This goes back to those in power who are fighting to stay in power, who maybe don't treat those "beneath" them very well, maybe they are cruel, or simply don't provide for others' needs. Their focus may be only upon themselves and they can't see any other way. They may feel their battle is to keep the masculine energy in control, though underneath they feel the changes coming. They certainly don't understand them, they don't want to understand them, but they do feel nervous, anxious, and worried, which leads often to overreactions from those in power, an overzealous need to control and be proven right. Narcissism and feeling entitled, often at the cost to others, is the norm, fighting to keep the male-dominated energy alive. The good news is that they will lose, eventually. The rising of the positive, caring feminine divine will see to it. As a male (in this life), I look forward to it, to the sharing and respect, and leadership of the female divine energy. The balancing of the energies will be a goal for those awakening to Spirit.

Patterns of Thought

The old thought patterns begin to shift; actually they have already started changing within you if you are reading this book. You are awakening from a long sleep, into the world of Spirit, which, of course, is where we all belong. We've forgotten, but now we see glimpses of why we are here on Earth, what we need to learn, and how to accept our lives as they are, rich with possibility and learning. Yes, we've forgotten, but our memories are beginning to come back and will continue to do so.

One of the biggest changes I've noticed in my own life is that I look at virtually everything differently. There is a different sort of life within all living things. Trees, flowers, animals, people, all are more magical, if you will. There is an inner glow or energy I've not seen since I was a small child. With this change I see the world is more alive than I thought, it is amazing! I now know that every person is here on the planet with soul plans, and they are all unique and interesting, every single one of them.

When you see others with this new insight, it changes the basic thought patterns you've developed your entire life. Small things are fascinating, the big worries sort of fade. What seemed so important in the past may not amount to so much now. You have changed just a bit and it continues to get better. I am not saying you became a monk or can now levitate, though I suppose that is a possibility; what I'm saying is that as you go about your daily life you simply see things in a different light. You begin to move away from judgment, from gossip and snide remarks. At first you go along with things, but as you awaken you begin to recognize what is happening, and the joke at someone's expense yesterday isn't so funny today. Yes, you will mellow a bit, but your positive energy will increase. Others will notice, though maybe not at first. There are those who will continue to fight the changes coming slowly all around them. But others will notice and you will be surprised at who mentions something of a Spiritual nature to you. Someone who you had no idea was interested in the topic. They are all around you and you don't know it, but they will show up.

What happens when you are living in Spirit as far as your thinking goes? Have you become brainwashed? No, simply realigned with your chosen path, a path that only you know and can choose. No one else can tell you what your path is for this life. So, back to your thinking—you will notice that a different picture forms in your mind when you happen on a situation. People may be upset for some reason, but you are less likely to judge them, instead you find yourself totally open to a caring approach, that they may have a good reason for their unhappiness and you respect that.

When you are living in Spirit you really approach everything in a little different way. You tend to see the positive in each situation and person you are faced with. You also understand that each and every one is a Spiritual person in this world for a short time, just the same as you. The bum on the corner, the CEO in the Fortune 500 business, the pastor at the local church, the policeman, the child living next door, everyone is an equal member of the Universe, and they are here for the same reasons you are here: to learn, to grow, to help, or to be helped. Remember, some souls volunteer to live difficult lives just to allow others to help them. The others are the ones who are learning, feeling compassion, and growing in Spirit. Often the person dealing with a crippling disease or injury agreed to go through the pain and suffering for someone else's benefit, an interesting concept that completely changes the way we look at those who may be dealing with handicaps of all sorts.

Again, you have to live it, internalize it, make it a natural part of your life by being authentic, by being open to new ideas, open to your intuitive thoughts and feelings. Learn to trust what you feel, which is a major step forward. Some have always trusted their "gut feelings" to guide them, and some doubt everything and second guess themselves regularly, which certainly can cause all kinds of anxiety. When you learn to trust your inner self you will begin to free yourself of much of today's angst. Try it and you will see.

Chapter 5

Moving into the Light—Acceptance

Close on the heels of awareness (always the first step) is acceptance. You've begun to sense things, to feel things, to have a glimpse of what seems to be the truth. You've known something has been sort of left out in your upbringing; at least there are a lot of questions you haven't been given answers to. The search has been pretty much left up to you; you are on your own. But there is something there. Maybe you've found a book, or watched an excellent video, or talked to someone who seemed to know what they were talking about. You've felt some inspiration of sorts, and intuitively know you are getting closer to making some sense of it all.

You've felt glimpses of intuition in your daily life, and maybe it has helped. Coincidences occur, but you look at them in a different light. Are they actually coincidences, or something else? For the first time you don't just ignore them, you observe them, and after a while they don't seem so haphazard. These little twists of fate you notice during the day may have something to them, like strings being pulled behind the scenes. Of course, you could easily ignore them, move on as before, but that becomes difficult, if not almost impossible once you've begun the awakening process. You will find yourself drawn back to these new thoughts again, and as you examine them, like anything new, after a while they begin to feel familiar, more natural. You've taken the first steps to a Spiritual approach to life. Not overnight, it may take years, decades, lifetimes, but you are changing, as are so many around you. As this inner feeling grows you question it less and less, and begin the next big chapter of awakening: Acceptance.

The Light

The title of this chapter, *Moving into the Light—Acceptance,* refers to the Spiritual light that fills us. That light is available at all times. Have you ever known someone who seems to be happy all the time, or at least most of the time? Someone who seems to have it all together and doesn't make a fuss over small things? They don't complain or get themselves involved in the middle of arguments or shoving matches, and somehow hold themselves together when turmoil is all around. Sometimes a person like that seems to glow from an inner energy. They may be filled with Spirit, and have moved into the acceptance phase. That is, they don't question everything so much, they don't look so hard for "miracles" and magic to happen. They know there is another side to life and they simply go with it. Like the Tao, they flow as a river moves slowly along on a lazy day. Nothing much seems to stop them. Something or someone may slow them down, but they deal with it and move on, or simply go around the obstacle. When we move into the light of Spirit we feel more content, and though there will always be challenges, we overcome them, realizing they are simply bumps in the road.

Keeping in mind that we are spiritual beings first and foremost, here to learn and experience life as humans in the physical realm, it becomes easier to accept that life's hurdles are just not that big, mostly. Yes, there are life-and-death issues to deal with, and all manner of injuries, heartbreaks, and so on, but again, these will pass. Well, except death. The final stepping stone through the veil is not the frightening, judgmental occasion we've been taught to believe. It is gentle, with loving hands waiting for us. We will feel we are finally "home" and wonder why we didn't remember this while on Earth. If we had remembered, everything would have changed. We would not have experienced the emotions and ups and downs of life, we would have been wise, knowing we would live forever. The "small stuff" would simply not concern us as much. In our egoic world we tend to make a big deal out of so many things that don't really matter. I like this idea: when something upsets you, ask yourself how important it will be in a day, a week, or a year. Not important at all in almost every case. You find yourself much less anxious and upset if things don't seem to be going quite right. You are aware there is a lesson to be learned, and you become much more accepting. This becomes a constant in your life, and though it can slip occasionally, you find you bounce back more quickly than before.

Sometimes We Need to Slow Down

Modern society is so go, go, go, that there seems little down time to relax and get our balance back. This leads to many health, emotional, and indeed, Spiritual issues. We can lose our way by being so busy. No time for this other "stuff"; we need to keep moving, checking our phone, or e-mail, our messages, and keep the social life moving forward. All so very important. Can't slow down, yet. Maybe later, like when I'm old! OK, that is a choice, but maybe a somewhat more rounded existence would be helpful? Balance is the key. There is time for all, but without the quiet time for the soul, troubles can easily escalate.

This is why I say we should move into the light. The light being the energy of the Source, or God. When we slow down, meditate, put time into positive thinking, we bring the light to ourselves. That light attracts other lights, and soon it grows and gains strength. You are never alone.

Many years ago, when I was about twenty years of age, I wrote the following, and I think it finally makes sense after rereading my last paragraph. We do attract what we are and what we believe.

Story of the Flame

All is Blackness.
Suddenly a candle flickers—then burns strong.
It is alone.

All is Darkness.
One candle burns brightly—he searches for other flames.
He finds many,
but all of them burn as though caught in the wind.
They flicker and die.

All is Blackness.
One candle, lit.
The melted and burned-out life of the others he ignores.
There is another, somewhere.

All is Darkness.
The straight, true flame thinks.
It is a long time before he finally realizes the light he
sees in the distance is a candle, too.
He has been staring at it for a long time,
but did not see it until now.
It is still a great distance away.

All is Blackness.
Two candles at a great distance do not share their light
or heat. They do communicate.
He stands up as straight and high as he can.
She sees. She is standing tall and proud, also.
He waves back and forth. So does she.
They are still far apart.
There is much space between them.

All is Darkness, save two specks of light.
He is rooted to a bottle, but his flame yearns to leap free.
He wants to fly. She is too far away.
She must be rooted in much the same way.

All is Blackness, save two bright specks of light.
Each candle appears to the other as a speck of light that
somehow expands with each passing moment.
They each have unspoken wants.
Who will light the way?

All is Darkness, save two small lights in the distance.
Fear that one of them might flicker and die
keeps them apart.
Are they afraid of the rushing air?

All is Blackness, save two small dots of flame.
Suddenly, as if upon a signal,
they both leap from the contentment of their wicks.
No more warm, molten wax to keep them from worry.

All is Darkness, save one flame, building.

All is Light.

© Daniel Bird

Always follow your heart. The idea of acceptance does not mean that you rely on someone else to tell you what to think and do. You will find those answers yourself, they will simply come to you as you grow in Spirit. You don't accept the teachings of others blindly, you find out for yourself. This is often the missing link in our development. Accepting others' truths may be easier than finding your own, but when you become more Spiritual in your life the truth will be there. You will know, and some teachings will mirror your own, but YOU are the one who found out, so it is real to you, based on your own experiences and feelings. I can't stress this enough: there are no shortcuts to Spiritual growth, they must be lived, individually. Working in groups can be helpful, and can help you gain an understanding, but ultimately the group can not move you along your own path. Their energy can help, but you do the moving. Accepting truths as they become known (and felt) by you will help on your journey immensely.

Moving into the light refers to finding the truth, accepting it in your heart and living that truth. The light is the energy of truth that radiates within you when finding your true path. The light is also the love of God or Source that shines as you understand. Accepting this light is our true goal and makes following our Spiritual path much easier.

Chapter 6

Working with the Ego

*A*hh, yes, the ego. Our friend, our enemy? Both? Our ego or conscious mind is always active, always thinking about this and that, with a couple of focuses: to keep us safe in our physical forms, and to keep itself alive. And how does it do that? If you are alive, isn't the ego there with you? Yes, it is, and by keeping you in a constant state of worry and anxiety the ego stays strong. It's both a necessary part of ourselves, and a challenge to keep under some sort of control.

I am not talking about the common concept of ego as in a boastful, self-absorbed aspect of one's personality. The egoic person who overstates and overestimates their own importance is related, but not in the Spiritual definition I am using. The ego I'm describing is within each and every one of us, and supplies the never-ending stream of conscious babbling we hear in our mind, which is actually pretty normal, but also fools us into believing all sorts of things that may or may not be true. Are we constantly in danger everywhere we go? The ego would have us believe we are. Paranoia is a tool of the ego, and fear. Fear is the biggest one. Anything to keep us on edge and concerned, even when there is no need for it, will strengthen the ego.

Why do I bring up the ego at all? Because it has a large impact on our Spiritual learning. The ego will often convince you that there are dangers, and have you nervous about the possibility that something will go wrong! This state of anxiety will bring more negative energy to you and can even result in the fear being realized. Being in control is important to the ego, and having it in charge will certainly slow down your growth. Now, let me describe what you can do, and how it all affects you.

Meditation. Yes, meditation. This is a way to control the effect the ego has on our lives. Why do you suppose it is so difficult to slow down the mind when we are not busy or when we try to meditate? Many people give up on meditation because they can't shut off the constant "noise" running through their minds. Ego doesn't want meditation; it pushes it out of the picture if possible. Meditation in its simplest form is quieting the mind, stopping the flow of data that never seems to cease while we are awake (and probably during sleep as well), to allow our mind to simply be, with no thought, no noise. I've mentioned elsewhere in this book that the quiet time is when our higher selves and our guides can communicate with us. Our human minds don't sense this—in fact, we don't realize anything is happening in meditation—but we often feel refreshed and better for having meditated. The communication that occurs between our souls and our Spiritual connections will then drift down to our conscious minds a bit at a time when needed. This would be like an answer to a prayer we've waited for. We really need to know something, like which job should I take? Should I move? Am I ready for a serious relationship with this person? So many issues that confuse us and ask us to decide. Sometimes we are ready and commit and sometimes we decide to hold off, it is not time yet. So we ask our guides and Guardian Angels and God to help. After a while we may see things in a different light and our mind is made up. If we can quiet our busy minds it can help with the "download" of information we may need.

You have been guided along your entire life and just didn't know it. Sometimes decisions you've made have worked out for the best, but sometimes things went badly and you've headed down a difficult path. But there are really no wrong paths, each way we go has valuable lessons, good and bad. Look for the positive in what you can learn! Then use that lesson to improve your life and to help with future decisions. If possible, look at every single situation you find yourself in as a wonderful chance to learn.

We Are Here to Learn and Experience Life

Remember, we are on the Earth in human form to experience that which cannot be experienced in our normal Spiritual form. Choosing to incarnate provides many opportunities to know life in the physical, 3D world. There is so much to do, so many places to go and people to meet, never a dull moment unless we want it, and that is just fine. We are lucky enough to be able to choose how we want to experience the Earth. There are some who travel all over the planet, learning about cultures and thriving with change, and others who prefer to stay close to home, leading lives that fulfill them in different ways. No right or wrong, no judgment, all choices are valuable and needed. Whatever you have chosen is right for you. However, let's say you would love to travel but can't seem to get it together to do so. You can never seem to get the time off from work or get someone to go with you, or it is just too expensive. There are a million ego-driven excuses for not living fully. If you truly want to do something, I promise your guides will help you find a way. You have to want it badly enough that the ego's excuses don't stop you. You want to go to Hawaii, have dreamed of that since you were a child. Ego says the plane might crash into the ocean! So you don't go, you don't take the chance. Besides, it costs too much. Ha! Excuses are everywhere! Do some research online and you can find tremendous bargains for staying in Hawaii or anywhere you want to go. And air travel is very safe, there are thousands of flights each day, but how often do you hear of a plane crash? It is more dangerous to ride in a car than on an airplane. If you can slow down your ego and convince yourself it is safe to go, and can make a plan to get the money needed, the time off, and so on, you will find the dream will become a reality. This has happened to me many times, and I've learned that amazing things can be accomplished if you move forward on your dreams and don't stop for all of the "can't" and "shouldn't" and "maybe someday" excuses that will come up. Stay positive and move into the "yes, I can" reasoning and the doors will open.

Victim or Learner?

The thought occurred to me recently that in every situation we find ourselves in there can be positive and/or negative consequences brought about by the choices we make. Ego pushes us, but our Spiritual side may push us another direction. We end up making our decision and moving forward (or backward). If it turns out the path was not a good one, we have no choice but to look at it and make a determination on how we want to think of it. Is it a good positive turn of events, or possibly a bad negative step? When you've decided that it was a mistake you have two main choices to choose from in your attitude. You can choose to be a victim (easy way out) or a learner, in which you look for the possible lessons present. I can't stress this enough: *every event that happens allows you to make that choice*: victim or learner. The victim blames everyone else, and of course the blame may totally reside with the other person(s). What if you let go of the blame game and simply moved forward looking at the lessons learned. No negative energy, that doesn't help anyway. Move on. Next time you won't be caught in the same mess, you now know to avoid it by moving in a different direction.

The Spiritual person is always learning, always seeing the other side of the coin, refusing to simply complain and do nothing. Even in the worse situations, learning and lessons are available. Every single one. By keeping our eyes on the learning aspect we continue to grow as humans and at the soul level. When something occurs that leads us to feel the part of the victim, it is useful to ask ourselves if this will be important in an hour, a day, a week, in our lifetime. Most often it will not be important for long. Learn from it and move on.

In some of the terrible situations we find ourselves maybe the learning is simply to move away from it. Get away, don't allow it to continue, find a way out, a friend who can help or at least listen. Change your victim stance to learner and move away from it. Remember, you are a full partner with your guides and God in this life and you deserve to be happy and healthy, but you are also responsible to make the decisions that will get you there.

Yes, the ego wants you to always choose victim status, so you can complain and whine and feel unjustly treated. It is so easy to be a victim in this modern world where oversensitivity has become almost the norm. Look at Twitter and Facebook, you can hardly find a positive tweet or status that doesn't have an answering negative comment. There are those whose ego is in control enough that they immediately feel the positive comment must be attacked. It is difficult not to want to fight back, but again, victim or learner? Refuse to add fuel to the fire and get into a back-and-forth argument. Remove yourself, or delete the conversation, or put an end to it. Sometimes trying to reason just doesn't help. Minds are not often changed. This is the world of social media at its worse. Of course, there is also the balance to that statement; social media can be used for great things as well. It is a wonderful way to communicate, to share good news, to share helpful and hopeful ideas with others; just be aware there will be the other side poking their take into much of what you post. Don't take things too seriously; that is the way of the ego and victimhood.

Chapter 7

Finding Your True Path

Why is it that some people seem to have all the luck? They may find riches, fame, fortune, and everything you could want so easily. You wonder what it is that makes the Universe smile down on them while you are working nine to five every weekday. Don't you deserve a break or two? Well, that is a great question, and yes, of course you do! But in order to see that happen you must line up intent, desire, and your beliefs the right way.

What does this have to do with your Spiritual path? Well, they are intertwined. There are certain skills and interests that we each possess, and we seem to burn hotter when we find ways to activate those skills and interests. An example might be a painter who finds a way to make a living creating watercolors and oils of nature scenes. This may be his passion, and the only occupation he can see himself in, so he puts all his energy and planning and studying toward that goal. He draws inspiration from inside and knows this is the right thing for him to do. The same could be said for almost any profession or career: auto mechanic, doctor, musician, writer, businessperson, and on and on. Your deepest interests (when you get away from ego a bit) can lead you to your Spiritual path.

Many people find themselves working in jobs that do not fulfill them, and they don't feel the passion or excitement they yearn for at the soul level. Some of them are miserable, some are trying to simply make it through, and some are working actively to get out of the situation and into a better one. This is human nature, and if you add in Spiritual nature you will be looking for the occupation that moves you the most, to the core. When you find this and actively move toward it, you will begin to find your Spiritual path.

Is it possible to have a job you dislike and still find your Spiritual path? Absolutely. What job you have matters not at all on your path, but it lines up and makes the journey smoother if you are creatively working with your passion. Combining your passion on Earth with your soul's desires creates a Heaven on Earth. This is what we are all striving for. Maybe it is a hobby you have that really gets you excited. The job not so much, but the hobby can sustain you. It is amazing how important it is to be actively moving in the direction of your passion! Even if you are not there yet, action toward the goals will see you through and prepare you for reaching those goals.

If you can identify what really makes you excited in life, you are ready to start moving in that direction. Pursue it! Stay focused, stay on the path, and ask for help along the way. Talk to your Spiritual Guides, ask them to help you with your goals. Put trust in their hands, and God's. After that, the only thing standing between you and your dreams is you! Of course, you won't have your desires simply handed to you. There is plenty of hard work to be done, and as you move along you learn everything you need to know, preparing you to reach those goals. Sometimes those lofty dreams and goals will change, and you will find something else that suddenly draws your attention. This is quite common.

Team up with Source, or God, or the Universe, and work with the energy that is available to you. Don't hesitate to ask for help when needed and trust that the best answers will come. God wants you to be happy and successful and will help you on your path. Turn over your worries to God. Put your request out there to the Universe (God) and trust in the future. Relax.

Your request can be anything, even something simple like wanting to find a parking space when they are scarce! Or you can go big, asking for a new job or promotion, whatever you want. If you live in Spirit, you will be surprised with the results. But it isn't because you "are living in Spirit" that it works this way, it is because you are aligning energy and vibration with the request.

Intent, Desire, and Beliefs

In the first paragraph of this chapter I said that to find your path you must line up your intent, desire, and beliefs the right way. If your intent is to become a teacher, say, because that feels like the most fulfilling career for you, then you must make the steps necessary to become a teacher. This would include getting the right grades to get into college, majoring in education, taking the classes, student teaching, and fulfilling all the requirements to graduate. Your intent is clear, but without the desire to become a teacher you may not get through it all. Desire and intent put you on the teacher's path, but do you believe you can be a good teacher? You need the belief to drive you through all of it. Intent, desire, and beliefs work together to get you to where you want to go, and if it feels right in your gut you are lining yourself up well on your path. Let me explain. Yes, I am talking about two things here: the path of your career and the Spiritual path. They are very much related, however. Finding the right career path, the one that makes you feel happy and fulfilled, puts the Spiritual path right in front of you. They are interconnected.

If you've always wanted to be a musician but your parents insist you go into the family furniture business, there is no time for music! This can leave you frustrated, and as you get bogged down with the store, and starting a family of your own, you get farther and farther from your dream. You can still have a wonderful, happy life, and your dreams may shift a bit, but if you had the chance you just know you could have been a great drummer. Your career path may have been pushed a bit to the side, but your Spiritual path will still be available. By the way, it is never too late to try something new.

The point is, you never lose your Spiritual path, it stays with you and you will find it if you make the right decisions. But when your work creates passion in your life your Spiritual path is so much easier to find, because it is often right there in front of you! Life can be wonderful and fulfilling. Find what you love, put your intent, desire, and beliefs in line and go for it! I wrote a song about the first visit I ever had with a psychic many years ago. I was quite young, but the lyrics are still true today.

Fortune Teller

[Intro]
I woke up and I felt so lost, but I knew I had to pay the cost
Since I just couldn't stay in bed I went to have my fortune read.
She dealt the cards and I looked away, looking back I was half afraid
Then I saw a smile creep into her eyes

[Verse 1]
Well, she drew the cards and let 'em fall
I knew then that she would tell me all … that I needed to know.
"Well, what's my future can't you see?
I'm not always sure what's right for me."
She said, "You know that's not true, it's all up to you. You've got to do something you love."

[Verse 2]
So I said, "What's on the menu? Can't you give me just a little hint?"
"Why is it that you must worry? Why do you have to question it?
Just suffice to say it's nice, you're gonna do something you love."

[Musical Interlude]

[Verse 3]
Suddenly I knew the answer. Get my guitar up there and play!
Look out with open eyes, I understood what she tried to say.
You know it's all true, it's all up to you.
You gotta do something
You gotta do something
You gotta do something that you love.

© Daniel Bird

What is interesting is that when I saw the psychic I didn't know what I was going to do with my life, but as verse 3 states, "Get my guitar up there and play!" and that is what I did. I found something I loved and was a touring, active musician for fifteen years before settling down, having children, and returning to college to become a schoolteacher. I recently retired from teaching and am back at playing music as my full-time interest. There is no describing the feeling you get when following your passion.

Chapter 8

Day-to-Day Life

What can you expect as a newly awakened person during your normal day? Will everything look the same, feel the same, smell the same? As a former professor in my undergraduate studies used to say, "It all depends on which side of the fence you are sitting on." I think what he meant is, who knows? Some do notice differences, some not so much, but here is the secret: it is all within. All inside. Your hands most likely will not tingle in some strange manner, and you won't be able to read minds, but you might feel a little differently about people you see every day. If you've begun the process of awakening to Spirit you can't help but see that those you are around are on their own journey, their own path in this life. Everyone is and you now are aware. This does change the way you view people. Helps you to be more patient, to understand, and especially to not take things so seriously. Life here, again, is temporary, and so much of what we've been led to believe is important is actually not.

An Average Day

Starting the day, you wake up in the physical sense. A great way to connect with the world coming out of sleep is to take a moment to orient yourself, and if possible, before you touch the ground, decide how your day will be. Yes, decide. You are the director of your life, the author of your story, and you can choose how each moment, day, week, lifetime is going to turn out. So before you pull your feet out of the covers, think to yourself something in the way of gratitude, and your wishes for the day. "I am grateful for this day, and wish to stay in tune with my own soul's guidance. Thank you." Something simple. But it sets the tone for the day and puts energy into action.

You can be as specific as you wish. Now keep in mind that saying, "I wish to receive a million dollars today," may or may not happen, depending on your plan for this incarnation, but you are free to think what you want. I choose to be thankful and open to what Spirit has in store for me. Once you have the energy started, you may find your usual dread of getting up and ready for work is a little less difficult. Our attitudes create our moods, and we are in charge.

Let's say you work in an office. Arriving at work on everyone's favorite, Monday morning, you say the normal "Good morning!" to everyone. Now, this is interesting, maybe you are one of those who rarely say anything to others first thing in the morning. If you are reading this book and it is making sense to you, I'll bet you do, though. Spiritual people are usually empathic, they feel in some fashion what others are feeling, or at least they are sensitive to the "vibrations" of those around them. You are now somewhat aware there are those who are happy to be at work this morning, those who are very unhappy to be there, and most are probably just there, not feeling anything particularly strong. I will repeat over and over that the first step in any Spiritual growth and awakening is awareness. If you are not aware of something you can miss it. You will learn as you go along, but becoming aware is always first.

The Workplace

Back to work. You have several calls to make, some forms to fill out, a meeting or two this morning, lunch with a coworker, and a rather lengthy report to be completed before you can go home today. A typical, somewhat stressful day. You can certainly put things off, skip making those calls, rearrange your schedule to have a long lunch, and leave the important assignments until later. This might work for you, but it certainly leaves the less enjoyable tasks for the afternoon when you typically try to slow down. After all, you are a morning person, right? Get some coffee and fire up the computer and you are wiz at your job! No one can hold you back. Unless you don't do those things and have a long lunch. Well, now you have a lot of catching up to do and your energy is a bit low. Being more aligned with Spirit might not make you a better businessperson, but it can help you with your focus and with understanding the choices you make. In other words, you can see that you are avoiding some things you don't want to do; after all, it's only Monday! Maybe a better approach would be to get the tough ones out of the way first, and try, if possible, to look at the tasks as learning opportunities. In every assignment you have to complete, you will find elements to support your Spiritual growth. Completing a task always feels good, and handling it up front sets a tone for your workday approach. Stay on top of the work, and your day is a Spiritual exercise, along with doing a good job in a fair and honest way. Your understanding of the way it all works is enhanced when you come with Spiritual attitude.

It's not the work, or the job, or the location that has the biggest effect in the office, it is your approach, from the big meetings to the smallest encounters with the cafeteria workers and the office cleaners. The way you choose to treat *everyone* is so important, as long as it comes from the heart. As you feel more in line with your path, you will see that each and every one of those in your workplace is the same as you; there are no higher-ups, no Grand Poobahs, in the world of Spirit. All are equal, and your treatment of each will reflect your awakening. As you begin to understand the world of Spirit, you will find yourself being kinder to all, and maybe talking more, being supportive, less competitive, more alive. Work no longer defines you, you define your work. In a few years, let's say, you have taken another position in another company. Will your former coworkers remember a great meeting you hosted, or a presentation you gave, or an excellent department newsletter? No. They will remember *you*. The you that they got to know at a non-work level. Not so much social, but at a gut level, what their own souls told them about you, or what they felt about you. That is how you will be remembered. The good you did, by recognizing them, by your concern, by your honest heart. Not how you loved to share gossip, or badmouthed the boss. Eliminate those things! Move away from the lower energy communications.

During a day at work you often find yourself bumping into someone in another department whom you rarely see. Always be aware that there may be a reason. Keep yourself open to positive interactions and energy. You may only say,

"Hello, nice to see you!" and that may be all they needed to cheer themselves up. If you feel like you should talk to them for a moment, don't hesitate; however, don't force it. You can read people pretty well when you are open to Spirit. Never be kind or friendly for reward, though. The idea of being extra nice to a department head *because* a job posting is coming up that you are interested in is disingenuous, it is not from the soul. Be honest and this won't be a problem. You may need to let them know you are interested, but keep it professional.

Gossip and Negative Energy

Yes, you will want to avoid gossip. This is very easy to say, and for many, very difficult to do. Anything negative said about anyone else puts out the wrong kind of energy. The energy coming from an office gossip is rewarded if others listen and contribute. They form a negative bond, one that can continue to grow as the opportunities for more gossip occur. This a good way to get attention, to share the latest "news" about others. It is attention, but not the kind you want! For some, negative attention is better than no attention, but it has to be fed by others or it will die out. Find a way to not take part. No reason to attach yourself to the negative energies involved, there is nothing good in this for you, or for anyone. Don't try to straighten them out too much, it can be frustrating. The main thing is to just not take part, and soon they will stop bothering you with it.

Keeping your energy positive will focus your attitude in the right way. If something has to be accomplished you really do not enjoy, look for the silver lining; it will be there, even if it is just a good feeling of having it behind you. Like attracts like. Positive energy brings in more positive energy. They reinforce each other. It doesn't take long to see where a person is coming from at work, or anywhere else. You will know rather quickly if they are mostly of Spirit or ego. The dominant side will show itself, but keep in mind they are on their own path, and change is occurring for them as well. We are all a mix of Spirit and ego.

Let's say you are waking up to Spirit and you see things differently now, you see more deeply, and understand that not everything is as it appears, so what should you do?

Tell everyone at work they are wrong, or at least confused? That you have found the answers, and are happy to share them with everyone? That you will be having weekly meetings during the lunch period for everyone to hear your wisdom? Well, no, you really don't have to do any of that. Of course, with free will you certainly can, but there is a pretty good possibility that you will turn off a lot of people. Unless they are at your level of consciousness, they won't understand and will most likely reject what you are trying to do.

You can go through your workday and do nothing. Yes, nothing! You still have to do your work, of course. I'm referring to wearing your Spirituality on your sleeve; it's just not necessary. Your actions will speak for you. Be yourself, and allow your new insight to lead you. Be kinder, gentler, and more understanding. Everyone is carrying their own burdens, with their own goals and challenges, and you should respect that. Allow Spirit to work through you, but in subtle ways, at least to start. A nice smile and "Hello!" to someone can start a chain of positive energy events, and if it doesn't it still adds the right kind of energy to the situation, and it can grow.

Driving or walking, riding a bus, however you get to work, provides a very useful time for getting your energy and attitude lined up with your soul's desires. If you drive to work each day, you probably have a pretty standard route you take, and after a while you see less and less of what is around you as you are driving. The drive becomes so commonplace and routine, you pay little attention. Your mind wanders, maybe it thinks through a problem you have to solve, or makes plans for some future event you are involved in, but it can be a very eye-opening time for you, going to or from work. As you awaken Spiritually, you start to see the people around you in cars, on foot, or riding bikes as Spiritual beings in physical (human) forms while here on Earth, just as you are. Look at them for a moment, see that they are just like you, doesn't matter the skin color, the kind of clothes, the age, or any other features. They are Spiritual beings. Could you just imagine our world if everyone could see this? If each person looked at each other person, recognized they are each children of God, and in fact are part of God? Recognize each other in the other person? Wow, that would be powerful. Who would want to hurt themselves? Who wouldn't want to help another on their

Spiritual path? A truly Spiritual world would hold its collective ego at bay and choose sharing rather than competition, love instead of hate, cooperation instead of war—if we could just recognize ourselves in each other. Seems so simple, but in our egocentric world it is quite a challenge at times, and for many it seems to be all the time.

Chapter 9
Staying the Course for the Long Haul

Each and every challenge faced in a day can be viewed as a lesson, a chance to learn something at the soul level. When problems occur look at your response, do you get worked up and nervous, do you get angry and frustrated? This was not what you expected, and now you have to deal with it. You get to choose your reaction, and that is very important. You hold the key, and the good news is that with practice your response can be whatever you want it to be. You no longer need to get upset or angry when things don't go your way, you can relax and know that everything is perfect, even though it certainly doesn't feel that way right now.

Practice. You won't shift, most likely in a day, or two, or twenty, it takes a lot of practice, and eventually you will respond with Spirit, the way of God, making the best possible positive energy choices. But, yes, it takes a while, and all depending on your path, for some it is easier than others. Fret not, there is no real hurry, the first step, as always, is awareness. Be aware when you are faced with a situation that *you can choose* to respond in a Spiritual manner, close to your own soul, and it gets easier.

Our lives sometimes seem pretty long, lots of time, and though that is a bit of an illusion, you will have adequate time to learn what you need to learn. Keeping your interest up in anything—a hobby, a job, friends, and so on—is not always easy. We tend to work in "waves" of interest, sometimes high, sometimes low, often in the middle. This will happen with your view of Spirit most likely, but as you incorporate the ideas into your daily life they will still work for you and you will make the right decisions, choose the right courses of action, and see the best in others. If you seem to lose interest (it often just takes a break), don't worry, it will return later on. When you feel the connection to your higher self, you will want to keep the positive energy flowing.

Cycles

The natural flow of energy, and indeed of life, is cyclical, with ups and downs varying constantly. Sometimes the cycles are a little shorter, sometimes a bit longer, but there is a flow that moves from high to low in a somewhat regular pattern. You are excited one day to paint the living room, but something comes up and you can't do it, even though you bought the paint, have the brushes, and so on. The next day looks to be a better choice, but you wake up and just don't feel like painting today. Interest, energy, and most everything else occur in cycles. Sometimes it is a matter of waiting for the right feeling or energy to complete a task. You can go ahead even on a down cycle, if you wish, but you will need to pull more energy into the task for yourself. At the high end the energy seems to come forth with little effort.

It works the same way for your interest in the Spiritual realm. It is not always easy to stay focused or excited. Don't fight it, and especially don't feel you are failing, or are simply not doing enough. You are doing enough! There is no need to force it, no need to pretend, to make yourself attend meetings, talk about it, read more books, etc., if you simply aren't feeling it. The interest will come when it comes, your higher self and Spirit Guides will help you. Let it flow naturally and it will find its own path, just as it should. Much like my favorite Spiritual image of life: water flowing down a hillside. This is like our life. It flows easily along with gravity until something blocks the way. Let's say a large rock is in the path. Does the water turn around and go back up the hill? Does it just stop and go no further? But life, like water, continues; there is more to it than one bit of water, more water is coming behind, much like life. So the rock will stop the flow for a short time, but as more water is added something happens. When enough water slides down the hill, it will follow the natural path and either go over the rock, around it, or even under it, just a matter of time and amount of water available. The water will find the most natural and least difficult way to continue down the hillside. It simply can't help it. Life follows the same path, there will be roadblocks, sometimes many roadblocks, but you choose how to deal with them. With anger? Angst? Violence? Or maybe with the flow? Step back, take a breath, look at the roadblock carefully, with open eyes and heart, and see the most natural way to move over, around, or under it. Allow your guides to help you. Ask them to help you solve the problem, remove the block, but be aware the issue may not move until you've completed some other task.

In other words, if you feel your path in life is to be a millionaire and you seem to be very short on cash, well, you can ask your guides to help with this, but it may simply not be your real path in this lifetime. Be aware of what you are asking for, be sensible, and then ask away! If your request is not in alignment with your goals for this lifetime they will probably not come forward, but the good news is that after a while you will realize this and learn acceptance.

No Need to Force Your Interest

Again, it is not necessary to force yourself to "stay Spiritual" but let it roll down the hill on its own energy. It will wax and wane, and that is natural, it is necessary. No one can keep up a single focus for a very long time without some kind of break, a lowering of the energy accompanying the task or interest. Don't sweat it, let it flow.

After we are first excited about our new ideas of Spirit and we find there are others interested as well, and it may be growing, we tend to find a lot of energy available. This hangs on for a while and we continue to feel this is something of value, and it may provide some answers we've been looking for. But after a while we find we are slipping a bit, maybe not as excited about attending a meeting or reading more on a Spiritually themed book. We just slow down for a bit. With newer awakening folks I have found that they then feel guilty, or that they are failing, that they are not worthy of this information because they are (temporarily) feeling less intensity. It is not a failing, it is certainly no reason to beat ourselves up and feel guilty! As I said before, it is natural for interest to rise and fall, and trying to make yourself excited about it doesn't work very well at all. So relax. If it is important for you, it will return.

Sometimes a person moves away from the Spiritual ideas they have been thinking about and discussing. They find themselves busy in the day-to-day world they live in, and the new thinking seems crowded out a bit. What I have found in my own life is that some of those ideas stay with me, I find that without thinking about the Spiritual lessons I've studied, they have found a place in my usual thinking patterns! This was a huge awakening point in my own life. For example, I used to see people out and about and find myself judging them, sometimes harshly for the way they looked, the clothes they wore, maybe the way they were acting. Now I find that I do less of that. I realize that I don't know their story. They are individual souls like me, no better, no worse, and we are together in this lifetime to have various experiences, which we share. This changes not only my attitude toward them, but my way of thinking. This starts to happen more and more, and becomes the norm. Studying, discussing, reading, and becoming more Spiritually attuned does change your life. You become more tolerant, more understanding, and a big one: less judgmental! You see yourself and others in a new light.

So, staying the course, even though it wavers, can have vast impact on your life. You will be focused, then off the tracks for a while, then back on, but you are subtly changing your life from the inside out, becoming more Spiritually led! Understanding this removes the self-made pressure and allows us to move within the flow of Spirit, and it grows as we accept it.

Chapter 10

Dealing with Others

Every single person on Earth is a child of God, a Spiritual being in human form for a short while. Every single person. People of all religions, and no religion. People of every color, size, shape, and background. Does not matter, all are Spirit, beloved by Source, and here to learn and experience life in all its forms. It is easy to forget this in our day-to-day encounters. An impatient driver wants to get around us on the highway, obviously upset we are driving the speed limit; an unhappy checkout employee at the store, who wants to be anywhere but here. Maybe we feel the same way. These are common ways to respond, not to say they are the best ways, but they happen. A step forward for a Spiritually focused person is the ability to not take such things personally, and see that outside events may have led to the behavior. By seeing others as they truly are we easily look past the temporary lower vibrations they are experiencing, and sometimes a positive response will lift them a little. Ask yourself when someone is upset and you are being drawn into it how long this will matter. Probably not long, and it doesn't need your energy input now. Accept and let it go, don't add to it. This lesson is difficult for some to learn, and we all slip up sometimes, but becoming aware of the situation and how the energy is added (or hopefully, not added) helps us decide on our own reaction.

We tend to want to lash out and respond to negative behavior with more of the same, to talk back, to yell, to let them know they are wrong. This becomes judgment. We have no right to judge. As I stated early in the book, we are each on our own personal path, with tasks and issues to overcome, sometimes including anger and rudeness. If we see others' behavior as lessons they are working through, we tend to be less judgmental and more understanding. Imagine if the entire world was this way! When many in the world are leaning toward the ego side of their duality, there is conflict. When the ego is in charge, power becomes very important—not power within ourselves, but external power, which is used to force others to reactions and behaviors of our choosing. Control is a favorite egoic goal.

Is the Ego in Control?

When ego is involved in personal relationships, problems may well arise. Arguments can follow, especially if both sides are egoic at the time. Both want to "win" and get their way. How do we deal with this from a Spiritual point? No one will win, first of all, even if one is forced into a corner and has to toe the line. Take for instance, a boss-employee relationship. The boss makes demands that the employee feels are out of line, the "It's not my job!" or "That's not in my job description!" kind of demands. The power is with the boss, and though he or she may get their way, no one really wins; there is now negative (slower) energy created between the two, which of course, attracts more of the same. So the next thing you know, you are complaining to someone else you work with, and they give their "supportive" tales and feelings, adding more of the negative energy to the situation. This can grow and grow until the workplace has become rather uncomfortable for all. This is a very common problem and it is sneaky. Comes up without you realizing it, and the wrong kind of energy grows stronger, making everything more difficult.

It can be difficult to walk away from this situation, you need to work, and though you are not happy with the arrangement, it can be beyond your ability to change it, so what can you do? There is really only one thing that can be done, only one thing you can change, and that is your own response and choice of behavior and attitude. You can refuse to drop to the level of gossip and anger, rather you can deal with it in a higher way. Again, ask yourself if this will still be an issue next week, or next year, or even tomorrow. Usually they are very temporary and will be of little consequence. If, however, you find that the negative egoic approach continues from your boss, and you don't deserve it, then it may be time to move elsewhere. Only you can know that. Sometimes the high road just isn't enough.

If we always recognize the soul of the other person, we will be able to respond in a positive manner. There are reasons for behaviors, and we may not know what is behind them, so awareness of the soul's search and lessons while on Earth changes our perspective. We tend to take disagreements less personally, we don't add more ill will to this discussion or argument, and we refuse to take on the issue with, or worse, for them. Staying neutral can help. Remember not to take it personally. Keeping your vibrations high allows you to float along above the fray and be less affected than those who are down in the trenches. Others will notice this, even though they may not be able to describe what is happening. We all know of people who seem to stay above the negative discourse of meetings. Have you wondered how they do it, or why? They may be attuned to the world of Spirit, and "listen" to their souls. Most likely they can't describe how or why they behave, themselves. It is not always a conscious resolve, sometimes it is out of their awareness; they just know that adding to a negative situation is not for them, and they are right. Remember, thoughts and words are real, and they stay around once created, combining with other thoughts and words, gaining strength. It is all energy or vibration. So choosing negative reactions does nobody any good. Of course, those who always seem above the bickering and arguing may simply not be paying attention!

Vibrations and Energy Are Key

You will find yourself in many situations in this lifetime that are uncomfortable, where you feel someone's anger or negative attitude. You will be in the middle of some of these and arguments will begin. First of all, as mentioned before, don't take things personally. This is a trap our ego often falls into, making it all about us and how wronged we are, or how wrong the other person is. If we don't take it personally and examine what the real issue is, we may simply decide not to own it, let the other person deal with it. Good approach, but what if the issue is directly related to you or your actions? You have to respond, but again, avoid making it a personal attack, find out what is behind the issue in as neutral a frame of mind as possible. Your ego would love for you to get angry, to fight back, or if you are a bit timid, to feel tremendous angst and discomfort. Refuse to go there as much as you can! Stay calm, breathe, and try to stay above it. If you keep your vibrations high enough, you can do it. Do not add negative energy to the situation. If the other person is angry and wants to argue, they are asking for more negative energy to be poured into the situation and you are the controller here, you can refuse to play that game. Refuse to argue and if necessary, refuse to listen until they calm down and can talk to you in a civil manner. You do not have to take it, you can put your foot down and refuse. "Now is not a good time, you are upset, we will talk about this when you've composed yourself." Let your positive self and energy take control and walk away.

Refusing to argue is not a sign of weakness; in fact, it is a sign of strength. It puts you in control and defuses the situation. Later, when the other person realizes you will not add to the drama, they will either have to come to you in a more civil manner or the issue will just dry up and go away. If you stay positive in your approach, others will gravitate toward you, you will draw them in. Positive energy brings in positive energy. You will be surprised by the number of people who are interested in not only the Spiritual aspects of life, but also by your positive, higher vibrations. They may not be able to put it into words, but they will be drawn to you. You will find that the Spiritual person is never alone. Not only do you have the discarnates around, but the living as well. By not letting negative energy overcome you, you keep calm and in control of yourself. Giving in and shouting might seem like a good idea at the time, but rarely will it have a good result. Most reactions and bad feelings reflect something from the angry or upset person. Don't take on the issues with them, or worse, for them.

One of the most difficult-to-avoid traps is gossip. Gossip lives in pretty much every work environment. The old water cooler talk, the lunch chat, the person who stops by your office to visit, many will be to offer some tasty tidbit of "information" that may or may not be true about someone in the workplace or that you both know. It is not easy to defuse gossip, but if you can avoid it, you are much better off. Don't talk badly of others; refuse to get involved in this kind of nonsense. It may be entertaining for a bit, but it just sets up a negative energy field that serves no good purpose for anyone.

Personal Power

You make decisions of all kinds every day, and some are small while some are large and important. But you are the one deciding, and you've probably given some thought to the consequences of your choices. Well, only you can really judge your actions and thoughts; no one else can do it for you, though there will be plenty of opinions! Make your decisions and move forward, stand by them, but be flexible and willing to change as needed. The point here is that you are in charge of your life, where it goes, and the steps you take along the way. By making your own decisions, you exercise your personal power, you stay in charge. If you find yourself accepting others' decisions for you, you give up some of your power. Don't misunderstand, getting opinions and the thoughts of others can be very helpful and lead you to the right path, but ultimately it is still up to you.

Personal or Spiritual power is very interesting, and some seem to have more of it than others. They often appear calmer, less confused by the challenges of their daily lives. Some people seem to flow through life more easily than others. Developing your own Spiritual insight and inner strength goes a long way in making your life less difficult to manage. Each decision you are faced with will have a new element included, that of the Spiritual angle, and it will influence your choice. This is a good thing, and might help you recognize the downside of some of the options, directing you to a better one.

Chapter 11

Guardian Angels and Spirit Guides

What is this "Spiritual angle" I mentioned in the previous chapter? Let me explain. As we awaken to the world of Spirit and begin to feel the input and impact of our Spirit Guides in our daily lives, we will add to normal daily occurrences the Spiritual aspect of each option we may decide on. An inner knowing, a little voice, helps us steer away from bad choices. We have an infinite amount of help from the other realm, guiding us when we ask. This is important, for the best results come when we ask for help. Our guides cannot interfere with our lives but can certainly help us see the larger picture *if* we ask them. They are available and willing to help at any time. I ask my own guides to help with my writing, with ideas, and with ways to be of help to the reader as well as myself. The ideas I share are directly influenced by my own guides, and their ideas are simply transferred through me as I type. My words, but they guide the input. I don't pretend to know all of this, but I have excellent help!

You have the same help available to you. We have Guardian Angels, Spirit Guides, and relatives and friends who have passed on the other side of the veil who will help when asked. Communication is very subtle at times and we must be alert for clues and messages, but they will be there. For me, often the connections come in my own gut feelings, I can just feel if something is right for me, or taking me off my own path. I have had this guidance since I was a child, though I didn't have a name for it or any idea how it worked. But I remember when I was about twenty-four years old telling my wife that every major decision I had made to that point had been guided from some other level outside myself, and I had trusted the guidance and it had proven itself and I was right where I was supposed to be.

Communication with Our Guides

So how does this work? Here is my take on it, and I am by no means any kind of authority. There are others who can tell you more. For me it has been subtle, but substantial. As I mentioned in the last paragraph, I felt guided through my life somehow. I always felt there was a higher power of some kind keeping an eye on me and helping me. I didn't question it, I just felt safe when making life-changing decisions, and so far they have been proven right time after time.

Maybe some definitions are in order. Some say that Guardian Angels and Spirit Guides are the same, some say they are not, that Guardian Angels stay with us for our entire lifetimes while guides change as needed. I don't know which is true exactly, but I feel there are multiple entities helping us all the time. I picture a small group of "souls" with one a focus point for my communication, sort of leading the group. This can be through gut feelings as mentioned before, or seeming coincidences that turn out to be very important or helpful. Like getting an unexpected paycheck for back pay just when your finances were in bad shape. These kinds of things happen all the time, but we may not recognize them as answers to our prayers. Our guides (including angels) are a sort of direct connection with God, and one of their tasks is to provide support for those on the physical plane.

My own direct connection with my guides came a few years ago when I went to see an incredible Spiritual lady who had the ability to see those individuals around you and communicate with them. I requested a reading from her and she agreed. Please note that she does not advertise, she does not look for clients, she does not offer psychic readings publicly at all. She told me that those who need her just seem to find her! So I asked for a reading and expected to talk to her for a half hour or so. Well, three hours later we were done! A three-hour reading! She said there were a lot of folks who wanted to come through to me and the information I received was not only fascinating, but incredibly accurate. She discussed many of my relatives who had passed in great detail with humorous things they said, which tipped me off to the authenticity of the reading. To say I was amazed is an understatement. I came out of there walking on air and buzzing with newfound energy! I was lucky enough to think to record the entire reading to go back over the information, and it is as vital now as it was a few years ago.

When You Are Ready

The point of this is that when you are ready a teacher will appear! She told me that I should keep a journal of my Spiritual thoughts and just let it flow. Luckily I was a pretty good typist, so I started right away. Well, it just took off! I worked on the journal every day, keeping it on my computer. After a week or so I noticed that I was typing faster and the ideas were just flowing from my head to my fingers, and even more amazing the writing started to take on a higher level of thought. I realized I was getting help from somewhere, and my gut-level reaction was that this was very positive energy I was dealing with; in fact, it was so natural that I just knew I had been drawn to a very important turning point in my life.

I shared some of the journal with my wife and some very close like-minded friends. They confirmed to me that the information coming was very useful and continued to encourage me to write. I've gone back and looked at some of them, pulled out sections, labeled them as essays and reprinted them on my Spiritual webpage (http://www. wakinguptospirit.com/). You can visit the page and read them if you like. Broken down by topics such as ego, manifesting what you desire, reality and fear, acceptance, and much more. So much information came my way so quickly that I had to go back and read the entry after I typed it to see what was there, and I was always surprised how easy to follow it was and how timely and useful.

I started asking my guides direct questions. Then I would wait a few seconds, put my hands on the keyboard and see what would come through. No, just for clarification, this is not what I consider "automatic writing" where some entity takes over your hands to write or type. For me, the words appear in my mind as I'm typing, and I often have no idea where the thought or sentence is going. I simply type the words as I "hear" them in my mind. I never feel any pressure or fear or anything but joy and the desire to help. I often go to my guides with personal questions now. They can help me find what I need to do, but they don't cause anything to happen, they just help me know. I just have to ask. By the way, there are times they won't come through with anything very obvious due to the nature of free will. We all have free will and can choose to respond to anything any way we want. Advice and suggestions are fine, but we ultimately make the decisions and go the way we want, whether good or bad.

Each and every one of us has this same ability, though like anything (singing, math, driving a race car) some are more naturally talented than others. Doesn't mean you can't do it, but it might take some work. I didn't know of my own connection until I started the journal. Hey, it might work for you, too! Keep in mind that there are many ways to communicate with your guides. Maybe through music or painting or being a good person. Spirit shows itself in every aspect of life, and tuning in to it brings it alive.

Chapter 12

Spiritual Skills and Talents

People around us have various abilities and interests; we are not all the same in this area. For instance, you might struggle to understand math equations, but you are a natural at solving plumbing problems. Or your friend can really throw a football a long distance with accuracy, but is tone deaf when he sings, while you are in a band, the church choir, and play several instruments. The point is that we all have our talents, often in very different areas, and this is true even within a family unit. Personal interests work the same way, one is very interested in sociology in college, while another wants to study agriculture or literature. It's lucky we are this way. Just imagine if every single one of us only wanted to study the weather! No one wants to do anything else! What a mess, but we would know a lot about rain and barometric pressure, wouldn't we?

Abilities and Passion

Finding your interests and moving in that direction is the way we find our core, our true desires, and like the saying goes, "If you love what you do, you will never work a day in your life," showing what passion does to the term "work." We all have talents of one sort or another in various amounts. Some activities are easy for you, but difficult for me, and vice-versa. We are not equal in talent levels all the time.

This is true of the abilities that psychics and mediums possess. They may be fortunate enough to have talents such as clairvoyance, the ability to see beyond the usual five senses, and maybe view the future to some extent, or clairaudience, able to hear what most cannot hear such as the voices of Spirits. Some can hold an object in their hand and get impressions of the owner and information beyond what the object would tell by simply looking at it; this is called psychometry. There are many others, and we all have them to a certain extent, and can develop them, but like singing or painting, we may be only able to go so far. Some are born with abilities that are well developed, some not so much. There are children who can sing opera and never had a lesson, but most children make due with "Mary Had a Little Lamb" or other simple tunes. The talent spectrum in all areas is spread wide. If you know someone who is gifted as a medium (can communicate with the departed) and you don't seem to have the gift, don't feel bad for yourself, feel good for their talent. Don't feel left out. Remember, we made plans before we were born into this life, and it is possible that one of your choices was to be at the low end of the medium ability spectrum. Or, possibly you are at the other end and can help many people with readings. Be happy with who you are and where you are in the talent scale. Remember, you can always work at improving your skills if you like. Meditate and ask your guides for help. They may lead you to an excellent teacher.

I, myself, have wished for these talents for many years, but seem to always come up empty when trying to use them, so I have just accepted this is how it is. But, as mentioned early in this book, I kept a journal and found I could type very quickly, in fact, faster than I could think of what to type. The words came along and I typed them up often not knowing exactly where the sentence was headed. I hear each word in my own voice in my mind as I type, and merely let my fingers do their thing. My fingers are not under anyone else's control. I have complete control at all times. I just trust the words coming up and go from there. I truly believe that these words and ideas are coming from a combination of my own higher self (my soul) and my guides. I've felt this for quite some time and have learned to trust the information they give me. It is a subtle talent, but one for which I am forever grateful! Usually after a writing session I have to go back and read what came out. Not that I wasn't aware of the content and wordplay as I went, but to get the real meanings, and to see if the words flow and are useful. In almost all cases I am surprised at how logical the words are. There are often words in my journal writing that I don't use myself. My wife has pointed this out before and told me that there is a different "voicing" in my journal than in my own writing, if that makes sense. She can feel the influence of my guides in the text. Amazing? I think so, and I've learned so much from it. I am always thankful for this gift.

Why Write These Books?

Some of the concepts from my first book have made their way into this one as well. I feel that the topics chosen are important enough to be reviewed, but the content has been expanded and hopefully clarified a bit. The first book was written directly for anyone just beginning the process of waking up to the world of Spirit, with questions that they may have. It was a gentle explanation of some of the feelings they were experiencing and really came back to the idea that this was all normal, healthy, and honest. The Spiritual teachings of our past have been sort of set aside by some of the religious orders and we are often not exposed to them. I feel that the Spiritual way of awakening, learning, and finding our own path is the most important information we can be exposed to. I felt like the information being transmitted through me was helpful and that I should make it available to those who could use it. Once the first book was accepted and published I spoke at several conferences, on a number of radio programs, book signings, and group meetings to explain why it was written. I have been very lucky in that my message, or rather the message of my "team" of guides and myself, has found an audience. I've been told several times that the content was just what someone needed to make sense of their own situation, and they felt relieved and validated! No higher praise could come to me; it was meant to be helpful, to take away any fear, and to tell everyone how normal it is to find oneself feeling there is more to life than the physical world. Because there is! A great deal more, and we are missing so much of it.

This book, the second, takes things a bit deeper, with a little more outspoken tone. The world seems to be a mess right now, but we can rise above it; it doesn't own our time, our minds, or our beliefs. We create our own world and can make one of positive energy with love all around if we wish. We are traveling on this big old bus (the Earth) together, and the more we are in tune with each other, the more fun the trip will be. With more and more people waking up to the Spiritual aspects of life, a change in the overall view of life occurs. We begin to see how much more alike we are than different, we begin to feel the joy and the pain of those around us, we find we care more about the levels of being. We share what we are learning (my books, website, music, and essays … www. wakinguptospirit.com and www.danbirdmusic.com), which helps to spread the word.

Spirituality Is Gentle

Yes, it is. Gentle, not in any rush, not forcing its way into your life. Gentle, like meditation is gentle, a quieting of the mind. Spirit flows through all of us, the energy is intertwined and moving, full of life. Flexible, constantly ebbing and flowing. Have you ever wondered why one day you are excited about something, the next day less so? One day you are full of energy and ready to go, and a week later you want to just stay in bed? The flow of energy like everything is cyclical, like the tide, it flows up and down, or back and forth. Nothing stays the same. Spirit does the same. One day you are excited about what you've found out, but a month later you have drifted, but it comes back. When something is real and useful it comes back. Something will trigger it and your understanding or interest will be stronger than ever. Spirit puts meaning into life and allows us to see more, feel more, love more, and understand more. Our lives become more useful and helpful. We think not so much about ourselves, but about others around us, and we help each other to grow, to learn, and to find God's path for us. It is all connected, and each and every one of us is involved. We each have our path, which intersects many other paths, and the crossing spots are interactions in which our free will allows us to choose what we will say or do. Or not say or do. It's up to us, but when waking up we see a clearer picture, we know our actions and words speak louder than we ever dreamed and that they have far-reaching effects. Our lives truly do change.

Chapter 13

The Big Picture

Awakening can change your life, but those who do not wake up to Spirit are just fine, too. It doesn't matter in the long run, because we will all get there eventually, regardless. It may take many reincarnations, but the end of the journey will come. So don't sweat it! Relax a little. This is not a race, nor a competition. If you are drawn to find your path consciously, do it! Enjoy and learn as you go. If not, simply go through life as you will, hopefully with love for others around you. It matters not if you are aware of your path and the obstacles, you will face them anyway.

I have noticed in attending some Spiritual discussions that there are always some attending who want to discuss the esoteric topics such as UFOs, string theory, Nostradamus, and predictions, and I notice that some people feel out of place. There's nothing wrong with any of these topics; they are fascinating, if that is what you are drawn to. The desire to study these topics is very strong in some folks, while others want to focus on improving their knowledge of a more personal, inner Spiritual direction. That is where I am. The soul-level workings of Spirit are important to me. What can I learn from meditation and study of the masters such as Buddha and Jesus? In some of these meetings (not all), the topic rarely delves into the personal level and how to improve and understand ourselves and our connection to the Spiritual realm.

Don't misunderstand, the other topics are interesting and may have significant importance, but having never seen a UFO myself, let alone Big Foot, I can't get worked up about them. I do see me every day, and I have the time to focus on my own Spiritual path. This is not to be confused with an egoic self-interest, but rather on the search within for the bigger picture. I'm convinced the truth can be found in each of us, and not as much in an "out there" focus. There is room for both, but the inner path is the key, at least to this author.

Moving from Waking Up to Living

We live in a physical, three-dimensional world, and are aware of what is around us by using our five senses. It seems that most humans alive today are limited to this level of awareness; they simply have not awakened to the world of Spirit. Again, that is all right, we are on our own paths. There is much more, however, than our senses allow us to observe. If life is like an iceberg, humans are often aware of the tip only (our physical world) and the vast majority remains just out of sight below the water (Spiritual world).

There are many ways to describe these "worlds," and comparisons are made all the time. In the world of science, dimensions can be described using mass, size, location, time, etc. Again we live in a physical, matter-filled universe, and many are comfortable with only that description. But there are some downsides to this limiting view. Within the three-dimensional world, there is fear. Lots of fear. Much of the world runs on fear and worry. Everything from war to simple arguments come from fear or the need for power, the need to be right at all costs. These are ego-controlled actions, not of the Spiritual realm, and their effect on many of us can be overwhelming.

Moving beyond the physical 3D world limitations is one of our aims; it allows us to shape our own environment. But where is this new world? What is it we are creating? Keep in mind that Spirit is within, the new universe is within, but the impact on our 3D lives is tremendous. Moving away from a focus on the physical world lessens a bit, and leads to the elimination of fear. Fear, after all, is the opposite of love, and is a strong controlling agent for much of humanity.

The first step to move forward is to change our old ways of thinking, to realize there is more to life than our senses tell us, or the newspaper, the TV, or the gossip we hear at the water cooler. We start to feel there is something we've been missing, something important, something deeply personal. As we begin to open up to Spirit, we start the journey to that deep understanding, to fulfill that missing need. It is right here within. That is how I view the next level. We are still here in our physical world, but we find an interest that leads us to questions, and a search, and we find like-minded people around us. This is guiding us into a world that is not ego centered, a world that helps us understand why people sometimes treat others badly, why countries fight, why Congress can't get along. These are examples of egoic minds fighting for their lives, to survive, to control. Spirit doesn't want to control, to argue. Spirit is love. The next level is all about becoming aware. It is the beginning of a path away from fear and ego's control. We are still living in a 3D world, but with a new understanding and awareness. The search for our Spiritual path has begun.

So there is more to it all than our senses can show us. We know that, but what is next? This is a big leap. You are now aware of ego and Spirit, and you feel that you are finding your path, that you understand more than ever before. The next level is living it, truly living in Spirit while still here on Earth. If you are reading this book, you are most likely drawn to the subject; if some of these topics resonate with you, you are growing Spiritually. You won't be able to see a physical change, it is within, but you have begun to awaken. Knowing about it and living it are a step apart, but a very powerful step. Living in Spirit takes away the "need" to be Spiritual, to think about what you "should" do, how you should feel. Those no longer matter because you are living from the inside out; in other words, your Spiritual side is where you draw your thoughts from, your guidance, and attitudes. You become the real you that you have always been at the deepest level. Your desires for possessions and money and power decrease, as does your need to be the winner all the time. You won't be drawn to violence so much in person, in movies, or in the news. You will see through all of that without a thought and likely feel repelled by it. A different view of the world has developed. You don't need to think about how you *should* feel or react to anything, you just move on through. This is not saying you don't have to deal with all kinds of issues, but your approach to problem solving changes. Your belief in the abundance of the Universe moves you away from the wants and constant worry of lack. Life truly changes, and you will begin to not only notice it, but to expect it. You have every right to live a happy fulfilling life, and when you move from awakening to living Spiritually it happens.

Waking up, becoming interested, moving forward, and as you learn you begin to move up the scale of Spiritual awakening. The greatest evolution of the human race would be if everyone woke up and followed their path. This is a great challenge as egoic entities will not be interested at the outset. Do not be discouraged. Remember your path is yours and yours alone. Move forward with faith and courage, the landscape will even out and become delightful, and the rest of the world will just have to catch up.

The World Today

I haven't dwelt on the current levels of upheaval throughout the world at the present time. Not that it isn't important, it is, but more important is how we choose to respond, how we choose to participate, if at all. The world is undergoing a huge shift in Spiritual energy and direction. The numbers of newly awakened souls are arriving for a reason. The "old" ways are being challenged. There is a certain new wave of thinking and feeling occurring, a Spiritual approach, though it very possibly is not called "Spiritual." The term does not matter. The reality of it does matter. So many are feeling that there have to be better ways of doing virtually everything! How to think, to live, to feel. Instinctively they know the system they've been brought up in no longer works, something new needs to come forth. And the biggest difference in approach is that they don't spend so much time looking outside themselves, they already know what needs to be done! Their Spiritual side is communicating with them at a higher level, though they may not realize it.

What we are seeing in the present time is an attempt by the past, ego-driven world to reassert itself, to hold onto control. This will not work, ultimately, as those who are awakening simply will not be under their domination. Once it is understood that real power is within rather than from outside ourselves, it becomes natural to see things as they really are. This breaks down the societal mores and opens up a new era of understanding. The egoic world has no place left to exist and exert power. When energy and knowledge are drawn from within, it is pure, it is honest, and it can't be commanded from outside. Jesus showed us this. He understood the human frailties and lack of understanding around him, and by his example and words he showed there is a better way. Jesus got his power from within, he was connected directly with Source, or God. By understanding what it was to be in human form he was able to show us the way to Spirit.

The pure words of Jesus of Nazareth ring true today. Unfortunately, some of his "truths" have been rewritten, changed subtly, or left out of the Bible completely. Instead of listening carefully to his words and following the ideas he put forth, a certain greed came upon some of the early religions and his words were changed. Jesus talked of the Kingdom of God being within. His life was one of good deeds, caring deeply, and teaching. Some of his words were changed or misunderstood, and man (in the guise of religion) saw that bending the approach a bit gave them (men) power. A great deal of power. Followers were told to listen to the religious leaders, that only *they* knew what Jesus meant. They were told that the priests have the power to connect with God, and that the people must work through them. A separation took place between people and God, there was a middleman. This is where things broke down. The connection we have with God or Source is pure, it is direct, and it is within each of us. We have no need to go through another person! But most of us were brought up thinking we needed that kind of guidance. Well, it allows someone else to do the religious or Spiritual thinking for us, doesn't it? We don't have to take responsibility.

There are many religious leaders, priests, rabbis, pastors, nuns, laypersons, and so on that are wonderful, caring people, and they are on the right path for their own souls. But there are also some who take advantage of religion for personal reasons, to gain power or riches. It is not right to judge them, but it is certainly right to move away from them. As we awaken, we see these things as they really are. Phoniness and dishonesty are much easier to spot when we think for ourselves than when we follow blindly. By going within (meditation) we connect with the truth, or essence of

God, and with our own higher self, our soul. Wouldn't it be wonderful if we had all been taught that from the beginning?

What Is the Simplest Way to Be "in Spirit?"

The simplest way is by being of service. This can be in your job, in the hallway, at the jobsite, in the factory, wherever you work, wherever you are. The happiest people are those who are of service, they enjoy helping others; they find a fulfillment in making tasks go easier for others. They are willing to take on some duties to help out. Being of service doesn't have to be only actual work details, it can be a smile, a positive energy, a word or two, and keep in mind that actions speak far louder than words! Small acts of kindness can have huge impacts! Never be afraid to be kind to everyone.

Keeping in mind that thoughts are real, they are energy and exist forever, thinking kindly of another is also being of service. Sounds simple and it is, but it is not always easy. Finding the positive within another can be a challenge sometimes! But always go back to the realization that even though they may not know it, they are simply children of God as you are, no better or worse at the Spiritual level. They are beloved of God and will ultimately rejoin all of us in the Spirit of Source. We will not fail, none of us will fail. But we move at different speeds with different goals and tasks to accomplish. Being of service is staying positive regardless of the situation. This is not always easy, but with practice it becomes a more natural approach and thought process, and we jump to conclusions less often before the facts, and move away from judgment. These are lofty but important goals for each of us.

Be kind. To everyone. We don't know where their path has led them or where it will take them next. They are learning (hopefully) their chosen lessons, and we can help by being kind. It creates positive energy, helps them along, helps us as well, and draws in more of the same, building in strength. This is why a group of like-minded individuals can become very powerful. The energy builds, and if it is positive it can do wonders.

Chapter 14

What Is Next?

Even after waking up and realizing Spirit is the center of all, we wonder just where we are heading in the long run. Well, of course, we will return to our Spiritual home when we leave this physical universe and plan for our next incarnation, if we want or need another one. "Old souls" are said to be at or near the end of their physical incarnations. They've done quite a lot and are ready to move on. You may very well be an old soul. How can you tell? Balance. Understanding, and a sensing of what is. Old souls may not be old in the physical sense, some are in fact children, and may seem wise beyond their years. Old souls recognize the truth quickly, and oftentimes have a hard time with nonsense; they are closer to their soul roots. They are not better or worse than anyone else; they are simply where they are on the path. This is not a race. We are where we are and should celebrate being part of God's universe, no matter where we are.

There are newer souls around, too, young souls who may not have the depth of being and knowledge at the soul level. They are all around us, too. All are equal in the sight of Source, and the journey is sacred to all. Do not concern yourself about that part of your soul, it just is. Be who you are, inquisitive, searching, asking, and experiencing life fully. Hurt no one, help everyone. Simple, but difficult directions sometimes.

The Future

For a moment let's think about ourselves, on this planet, at this time. What can we expect ahead? There are many options and choices to be made by all and we will just have to see, but I think the future, though very bright in the long run, may have a cloudy difficult time of it for a while. This has already started. I wrote earlier about the changing of the ages, the balancing of the male and female energies, and the resurgence of the divine feminine in our world, and this has started. You may have noticed more female world leaders, and a slow building of women CEOs and politicians. These are wonderful changes and necessary to help balance and save this planet. We need the feminine energy to balance a world that is off kilter at this time. The male dominance has led to war over and over, and peace is badly needed. Balancing the energies can accomplish that over time. But there is a battle to be fought, unfortunately. A battle to keep the old ways in power and control. This is being fought out in front of us on the news every day. So many people are seeing through this now, and more are growing up around us. Those who have awakened see the tragedies being acted out in the world, and they will demand change. Again, this will take some time.

Money and power and the war machine will slowly lose. When fear no longer controls people—fear pushed by the leaders and those in power—a change will begin. Fear is their biggest weapon; it keeps us toeing the line, it keeps us reacting to the possible dangers all around us. So we are asked to stand and fight! But fight who? And why? We are not supposed to ask, just do as you are told because it is quite dangerous and our way of life is threatened. So they say. I don't want to go into the negative energy this all pushes out, but it has to be explained a bit. As we wake up we ask questions like I did when a child when I wanted to know why a priest could forgive our sins but we couldn't do it ourselves. Weren't we created and children of God just as he is? And why couldn't women be priests? And why couldn't priests and nuns get married and have families? Well, they would be more difficult to control I think as their thoughts would turn to their children and spouses more and more. Control of married priests and nuns would be much more difficult.

The questions likely to come up now would be along those same lines, but even more intense: why are we fighting in this foreign country? To protect our liberty we are told, to keep America safe! But the country we are sending our troops to is thousands of miles across the ocean; how does this protect our liberty? We are told because it does. War has to do with money more than protecting us, at least in our country at the time this book is being written. We want to see what is behind some of the actions our government is taking, we want to know the truth. As we wake up our need for the truth becomes strong. In the past we took their word for it, we were asked to be patriotic and not question it, but we will outgrow that form of control, we will demand to know, and the battle will be to keep us under control and quiet and it won't work. I'm not saying we will rise up in a bloody coup, but we will make demands that truth and fairness rule, that honesty is in the forefront. Waking up Spiritually clarifies so much, and this is frightening to the old ways. Maybe the world will become filled with conscientious objectors who refuse to fight wars that make no sense, that don't benefit anyone but the war machines and persons in power. Wouldn't that be something?

The struggle for power has already started. In fact, it has been ongoing for thousands of years, but it may get more intense. The old ways will try every trick in the book to remain in control, but they will fail. This is happening now, but it will end one day and a new age will be upon us. It make take some time, years, decades, maybe longer, but it will happen. Books like this one don't simply show up, they are "commissioned" by a higher power I believe, and more people are moving in this direction every day.

Earth Is a Wonderful Place to Live!

This is a beautiful world with wonders galore. There is enough bounty to feed the world, to make it a safe haven for man and beast alike, but first we must make it through the turmoil and face the changes. With the lifting of the vibrational energy of our planet that has begun, the old powers will double their efforts to hang on. They will fail, ultimately, as grace and love will combine with the positive energy that we will provide to reclaim a planet of happiness. Spiritual people see the beauty around them, so if you appreciate the sky, the white billowing clouds, the cool breeze, or the seashore, the mountains, the changing colors of fall, anything you find beauty and peace in, then you are waking up to the Spiritual energy within you! You are on your path and have begun to identify the wonderful parts of life. This will grow as you continue, and make your life a Heaven on Earth if you let it, despite the confusion and angst all around you. One soul at a time, one person at a time, will wake up and join with others until the world is simply overrun with like-minded Spiritual beings in human form. Then we will see the true world evolve. Mother Earth will calm down, she will feel the changes, and she will welcome us with open arms again.

What can we do now to help move the changes along? Be open to ideas, be fair minded, avoid arguments and negative energy, remove yourself from those who want to be upset about everything. Observe yourself; where do your thoughts go when a problem arises? Can you keep from anger and lashing out, and if not, does that help the situation? Probably not. Calmness and care rule the day. Start with yourself, set an example. You don't need to preach on the corner. You can be who you are in the sight of God, the perfect soul inhabiting a human body for a relatively short time to learn and find out what it is like to feel the pains and emotions of this world. Lessons of all kinds are available and there every day.

There are more Spiritually minded people around every day; they are coming from all directions. You may be surprised by how many of your friends, relatives, coworkers, and neighbors are waking up. It certainly caught me off guard. So many have approached me since I wrote my first book expressing their feelings about it and thanking me for explaining some of the Spiritual ideas they had felt but didn't have the words for. That was my task, to make these ideas meaningful for all of us "newbies" just learning about the world of Spirit.

Never forget, however, that there is no us vs. them in this scenario! We are in this together, including even the most anti-Spiritual folks out there! Their time is not yet here, and maybe they volunteered to be just that way to help others wake up. They may seem to be very angry and to be fighting us, but what if they agreed to be on the opposite side, so to speak, which would lead to others questioning their thinking? They could be performing an excellent service for the rest of us, so do not judge. Difficult, we were pretty much raised to evaluate everything, weren't we? You can learn to catch yourself when starting to make a judgment about someone and move past it, drop it. After a while, you do this more quickly and automatically. This is one of the skills Jesus showed us, to not judge anyone! We don't know their story and if we did it would not make a difference, recognize their soul within!

I would also like to remind you, the reader, to do your very best to not judge yourself. On the soul level you know what you are about, and where you are going, and in our human forms we tend to not treat ourselves fairly at times. Forgive yourself each day and try to do a little better. Be kind to yourself regardless of your failings. We learn so much when we don't win. I've heard it said that we learn more when we fail, and there is truth there. Then we must pick ourselves back up, dust ourselves off, and get back to work, knowing we now have new knowledge and experience to help us in our next challenge. It is ongoing, and if we can accept the problems that come up and learn from them and move beyond them, we are all the richer for it.

Chapter 15
Living Your Life

A number of times in talks I've given, in essays written, and in my first book I've made the statement that "none of this really matters." I seem to contradict myself when looking at the content I've made available. Am I saying that I have written books and all for something that is of no value, that truly doesn't matter? No, that's not quite what I meant. Let me explain.

Spiritual knowledge is very helpful, and it can guide you on your path, help you avoid mistakes and pitfalls often made during a lifetime. An understanding of the Spiritual nature of all people may lead to treating others in a different, hopefully better, way. The influence of Spirit and God's love will move you in a positive way. But can you have a wonderful Spiritual life without this knowledge? If you had never read this book or any others on the topic, if you hadn't talked to anyone or watched videos or television programs, could you still be Spiritual? Could you be all you could be? Would you be fulfilled? Love this question!

Yes, you can be fully Spiritual without any knowledge of the topic whatsoever. The knowledge I share is not necessary, this book is not needed, unless you feel it can be helpful. If you are drawn to this material, it can be very useful, but it is all right if you don't feel drawn to it or have any interest at all. The real sign of Spirituality is how you treat yourself and others. Simple as that. A person can go through life respecting others, treating them fairly and with love, be helpful and kind, and know nothing of the soul, or Spirit, or the continuation of life after death, none of it! Doesn't matter. We are born with certain tasks and lessons to be completed, whether we believe any of it or not. Our souls know what we are here for, what we are trying to learn, and where we are being led on our path. Our human brains do not know, and that is part of the mystery of life. All of those tasks and lessons will occur during our lifetime. How will we react? What will we learn?

So why do we need to learn any of this? We don't. But if we are drawn to it, feel energized by it, and feel it enhances our lives then we can move forward. If we feel curious, find it interesting, and it makes sense to us, we can learn more about it. If we don't feel the need, we can simply move on with life, knowing that we are all perfect, and will be together in the end regardless of our beliefs. Free will allows us to choose what we want to learn and focus on. There are no set rules for how to live our lives. We are basically making it up as we go, finding our way through an often-confusing world. There is no right or wrong here, there simply is what is. Can I prove that we live on after death? No, but I have a strong feeling it is so, it just makes sense to me. Is it OK to follow a religion? Yes. Is it OK to not follow any religion? Yes. Is it OK to be an atheist? Yes. Is it OK to hate people? No, it will lead to more lessons for you in future incarnations. But you have the free will to hate if you want to. You get to choose. But, there is always karma to consider!

Each Day Is New

Every day we have a chance to regroup and realign our lives, we can turn the direction if we wish, we can change anything we want. We hold ourselves back more than anything else. Maybe you want to live a simple life, of no trouble to anyone else. That is your choice, and it is all right. Only you can decide. Some people are ambitious, some are not. Some want to change the world, some do not. We are an amazing blend of souls inhabiting this Earth, with similarities galore, but with many differences as well. The differences are far fewer than the similarities. We are human, we have a soul that lives on, and we are here for a relatively short period of time.

Each day we can make a difference, even if it is very small. Today I will pick up that piece of paper on the sidewalk by work that I walked by the last couple of days. That sets up the first tiny step of positive energy. Who knows what you do tomorrow? Hold the door for someone, say hello to a stranger, maybe even make a new friend? The opportunities that come to us each and every day are uncountable, they are vast, and we simply need to open our eyes to see them. Kindness and love make the world go around, it is that simple. Our souls know what we need to do, and I promise you they want us to live with kindness and love. Love is the highest vibration!

Will we slip up sometimes? "I just don't know if I can be kind all the time and love everybody." Of course, we will slip up, that's a big part of being human, but what can we learn when we do? Lessons are everywhere. We might make a hundred mistakes a day, but are they really mistakes? We might think so, but they could also be reminders of what we can change for tomorrow. Let's say someone cut you off in traffic on the way home from work. You are tired, just need to get home, and so you get angry; after all, you've waited your turn, and they just jumped in front of you! Not fair! So you yell at them, maybe show them a rather long middle finger, all because you felt you've been wronged, treated unfairly. This is very common. What can you do about it, though? As you drive on, you might realize how unhelpful your reaction was, in fact you feel badly, that isn't the real you, you don't do that sort of thing! It happens. Move on, learn from it, and the next day, if it happens again, you may recall how you felt yesterday, not so good afterward when you let your temper get the best of you. Today you simply move along, not happy at the other driver's action, but it doesn't get to you the same way. You've learned something about yourself. This is growing Spiritually. I don't mean to say you roll over for anyone who wants to push you around, but you look at the situation clearly, with open eyes, and you are able to predict how you will react, and that is what you can control.

Your Life Can Change

From my own experience I can tell you that opening up to Spirit can change the way you approach life. You see the other side of things so much easier, you step away from judging others, you accept the good with the bad and learn to deal with them both. When you are about to react to a situation your higher self reminds you of what you've learned before and helps you make better choices. This is powerful stuff!

Yes, you will feel you've messed up at times, maybe often, but you are moving forward on your path. You are making strides to find your true self, the self you've forgotten when you became a physical entity. It is not always easy, but it gets easier as you move forward. You gain inner knowledge that helps guide you. You see the good in others much easier, and you want to emulate that goodness. No longer do you wish to do harm or create any kind of negative energy, and you learn to reject it. You have a conscience that guides you that is working closely with your higher self, your soul. This allows you to stay on the desired path in this lifetime and to learn your lessons. Life becomes easier.

I have found it interesting that as you awaken you take things less seriously. You enjoy life and don't get as shook up by events. Life is temporary and as you look around, you ask yourself what is important here. Most of it is not, but the life we lead is. Material things are of little value. Yes, of course, you need the necessities: food, water, shelter, clothes, safety, and so on, but what we often consider important can actually be distractions from our real goals. More and more money, cars, possessions, power? Remember, you can't take it with you, so what good are they in the long run? Some feel they are worth fighting and even dying for, but are they, really? Not so sure.

Our daily lives are full of angst—from difficult bosses at work to long commutes to get there, to the news updates which are almost always bad, and a million other things pounding at us. Learning to ride above it is another of the wonders of awakening. A clarity of what is really important comes to you. You learn that these things don't need to affect you so much as before. Most of the problems of the day are minor, often not worth the trouble of getting angry or upset. For example: you walk out the door of your house to head off to work and realize you forgot your keys. A quick reaction is to cuss and get angry at yourself. You have to go back in the house, get the keys, and then return to the car. What a big hassle and waste of valuable time! Or is it? I do this kind of thing so often that I'm teaching myself to laugh. I usually say, "Of course!" then shake my head, smile, and go about my business. That is the reaction you can learn to bring forward, and it keeps you calmer and happier. What is it they say, "Don't sweat the small stuff, and it is ALL small stuff?" Something like that. It is true.

The big picture of our lives from the Spiritual perspective helps us realize how trivial some things really are, and we can move past them much more easily. It changes everything. You may not be dancing around all day, but you have an inner strength that maybe wasn't there before. Life is a wondrous thing, and though I believe we live forever in the Spirit world, the time here is precious. Discovering all that the three-dimensional world has to offer makes for an amazing trip. Appreciation is another sign of waking up. We see things differently than before, we notice details in nature and beauty that were there all along. Don't let your ego get in the way of your discoveries, and it *will* try. There are always worries to be brought forward, and those will slow down your Spiritual view of the world. It is a magnificent place no matter where you are on the planet. Try to visit as much of it as you can, or even search around where you live and you will find so much more than your realized. Even in your backyard!

Chapter 16

Joy Is the Goal!

We have many challenges in our lifetimes, ups and downs, happiness and sadness, and everything in between. But I will let you in on a little secret: the key ingredient to living your life successfully is JOY! A life full of joy. We have lessons to learn, karma to balance, and all of that, but did you know that you have total control of your life? Maybe not some of the things that happen around you, but of your actual life you are in charge! Your attitude is the key. You get to choose how your life works out and you can decide at any time that joy and happiness and gratefulness are your focal points, even when things go awry. Like the silver lining in the dark cloud, you can find the joy within life's turmoils.

There are rich people who are unhappy. They have everything in the material world that their hearts can desire, but some remain sad or incomplete. There are also very poor people who live happy satisfied lives, even with their daily struggles. They do not allow those problems to affect their outlook. Somehow they manage to accept their situation and keep their attitude positive. I'm not saying all poor people are happy, or that all rich people are unhappy, the point is that the material world doesn't have to own you; you do not have to buy into the fallacy that more money, cars, homes, boats, etc., will make you happier. Might entertain you for a while, but owning more stuff will not fulfill you inside, at the Spiritual level. This is why some wealthy people are sad; they want more and more, yet are not feeling better as they get more and more. What they are really yearning for, but don't realize, is Spiritual in nature. There is a confusion between material and Spiritual riches. In our world this is rampant. Greed is very strong. Our society worships money, and these are all challenges to Spiritual growth.

There is nothing wrong with money, or cars, boats, and all of the things money can buy; the issue is in the desire. If my strongest desire is to get more money, over all other desires, I may struggle with my Spiritual path. Do we have to focus only on our path, then? No, of course not, we can continue with our normal life, but being aware of what our heart is asking for will help guide us. True happiness will be found within, not with material objects or power, those are not where true power comes from. Always look within for the truth and the connection to who you really are, not outside. This is a huge lesson to learn, but you are reading this and you probably sense this is true.

But How Do We Find Joy?

How? By being honest with ourselves and others, by looking within in meditation and asking for guidance. By making ourselves smaller. Smaller? Well, let me say it another way: by moving our focus in life to what we can actually change. Becoming aware of the wonders around us, simplifying. The best way I know of to find pure joy is to remember what it was like to be a small child. Get smaller by actually getting down on your knees to look at plants and flowers, to play with the dog and cat, anything that reminds you of the wonder of the world when you were small. I remember clearly finding a small area of dirt in the yard when I lived on a farm in Iowa at about age seven or eight, and with my brother, Steve, we made roads in that dirt about two inches wide, and streets, and then played with our little cars and trucks. I remember it as if it was yesterday.

When you are a child you are closer to the ground, you notice things more, and you are also closer to your heart's desires, probably because you've not had to carry around a long list of adult worries yet. I remember honeybees floating by, and watching them land on flowers, and all manner of insects living in a small world that must have seemed huge to them. When you start to recall these things, you feel the innocence and simplicity of childhood, when living was untainted, pure. These kinds of feelings can be nurtured, and they will enrich your life. I am not saying you need to return to childhood, no, it's too late for that, but why did we let the wonder of childhood dry up so much? Some people never lose it, and those are the lucky ones. However, we can all learn to feel it again. It's like reconnecting with Mother Earth, with the planet that makes our human existence possible. The Earth truly is our mother, and we often take her for granted. Damaging the planet for profit is unforgivable; looking at short-term gains while ignoring the distress and injuries to our home in the long run is shortsighted.

Respect is needed, and it is coming with the shifting of energy that has begun. Better times are ahead, but we must endure the fight for the old ways that will try to slow the shift.

So we should start slowly, and get small. Look at the changes we can make in our lives, learn to feel the guidance that is available, and ask our guides to help us find our way. With the number of awakening individuals increasing at a high rate, it is just a matter of time before the new age becomes obvious, even to the naysayers. It has started and that is exactly why books of this sort are becoming more common, why someone who never dreamed of writing a book would do so. I felt driven to write, to share the thoughts and ideas I had access to from my guides. I am as surprised as anyone else that this would happen, and it fills me with happiness and gratitude. When it comes to my own Spiritual path, this is in the right direction. But how about your path? Maybe you don't feel the desire to write, in fact, feel no need to do much of anything about your path. That is fine, you will know in your gut if you have a task to complete. It might be something like raising children; get them through school with your guidance and turn them loose as young adults. That may be your task. Or maybe you agreed in this lifetime to have a simple, easy life in which your goal is to stay positive around others, and by doing so set an example. There is no need to put pressure on ourselves. Our path is there, and when we find it we will know. Often it is exactly where we are, and if we are making a wrong turn we will feel it. Then we redirect.

How Serious Should We Be about All of This?

It is easy to begin the process of waking up Spiritually and then take it very seriously. Serious to the point that we feel we are failing. We aren't "Spiritual" enough! We don't constantly feel holy or enlightened. No, probably not. Remember, you are human and will probably struggle with the image you've created of what you should become. Feeling we should be more than we are is a dead-end street. Acceptance is what we want, acceptance of what we are, where we are in our paths, and where we are going. This doesn't mean we don't strive to improve and want to be better, but creating an unrealistic ideal of our new improved Spiritual self can lead us to frustration. Enjoy the trip, the growth as it comes, and the journey!

I'll admit that when I began this awakening in my own life I thought I would see angels soon and hear my guides talk in regular voices! It didn't work that way, and I was feeling like I missed the boat somewhere. Others that I knew had those abilities, but I seemed to miss out. It took a while before I realized how different we all are, and our tasks are different from one another, as are our skill sets. I could write with input from Spiritual Beings! This was an ability that snuck up on me, and I didn't even know I had it for a long time. Once I understood, I got out of my own way, gave up wanting all these esoteric abilities, and learned acceptance. I'm much happier.

They say anyone can do these things and everyone has the ability, but anyone can also play basketball, can anyone dunk the ball? Nope, only those who are tall enough or have tremendous jumping ability. Most skills are like this, so we should accept where we are, though continue to work toward improvement. This is not a race, there is no need to be jealous of another's ability (though it seems to be quite human to feel that way), and if you are gifted in some way, don't show off, or try to make yourself important because of it. I have attended Spiritual discussion groups where a couple of those attending decided they should try to one-up each other with their knowledge and experiences. This really turned the other attendees off, especially as it continued for a while. There is no competition in Spirit! When that attitude appears, we need to slow down and reevaluate what we want out of it.

If a person is gifted in a psychic way, does that make them a good person, or a bad person? They can be either, or somewhere in the middle, just like all of us. There are talented mediums, for example, who are not necessarily nice people, and there are plenty who are wonderful; it covers the full range. The point is, if you know someone who is psychic and gives readings, they are still human, and they have all the foibles and issues the rest of us have. If they are successful in the business side of their psychic work, they may find that the money and fame starts to affect their view, but this happens in any business that is successful. Some don't change at all, some do; just be aware of it. Always remember we are human, and that alone is a challenge!

Awareness and Acceptance

Two of the most important "A" words involved with Spiritual growth are awareness and acceptance. Before you can accept the new concepts, you must become aware of them. Many of you reading this book are aware of much of what I've written, and some of you are not. This book will help with the door opening to awareness. That knowledge can then be accepted or rejected. But what if you don't accept these ideas? That is OK, you are still here, on your path, and the opportunities for growth will still be here. It's like going to school where we learn concepts first, then apply them to various situations or problems. Once the awareness is there, it can lead to more interest and energy put forth to learn. See it, feel it, sense it, and then accept it. I don't know how many times over the years I've come back to this, but it is an important common thread to moving forward for me, and for you. Accepting what you learn, accepting what your gut or intuition tells you, is how you learn to move in the right direction.

Following acceptance is growth. Growth of the soul, of positive energy, of knowledge that encompasses a bigger picture. Lives become more meaningful, people become more than strangers, we see them as souls like ourselves. Our prejudices lessen, we are slower to judge others and slower to judge ourselves. Life has a different light, the view is a little clearer.

Chapter 17

Some Final Thoughts

My books are not complicated or very long. I try not to preach or push ideas on the reader. You are welcome to believe or not, to accept or not, your path is yours alone. I try to use language in the same way I talk to people. I don't wish to confuse myself any more than necessary! My books reflect what I have felt and lived in my own life, and there is nothing here that isn't available to you, and even more. Some concepts I've repeated in this book; these my Spirit Guides feel are most important for our human incarnations.

The basic ideas are simple: don't sweat it, be happy, find your path, and move forward. Do you need to know all of this Spiritual stuff? No. Can it be useful? Yes, if you are drawn to it and it feels right. Is it necessary to know this to lead a Spiritual life? No, you can do that on your own. Your higher self (your soul) along with your Guardian Angels and Spirit Guides will continue to guide you no matter what occurs. You don't need to make any effort at all if you don't wish to. Simply not needed. If you want to, that is great, but no pressure. Life on Earth is to be lived and experienced. As more people wake up and feel an interest in finding out more, they will be drawn to books and videos like this, and find people who feel the same. I've seen an amazing growth in the number of folks waking up in the last few years. They are all around, some are friends, relatives, coworkers, and neighbors. Social media, web pages, Facebook, and Twitter are great ways to find like-minded individuals. Find discussion groups and attend meetings if possible, if you wish. There is a great deal of interest and content available all around us now, and I expect it to continue to grow. I truly believe it is the open mindedness and awareness of the Spiritual community that will save the planet in the long run, and many of those folks won't even know they are Spiritual in the first place! What does this mean?

Spirit comes from within, not from books, television, or even groups and friends. All of those can help you on your way, can make suggestions on how to learn, share their experiences with you, and offer guidance, but as I've said before, it comes from within yourself. Without that key element you are following someone else's experiences. Again, you don't have to meditate or do anything at all, but allowing your inner self to communicate with you in hunches, intuitive thoughts, or just guessing can lead you in the right directions in life.

The World Is Changing

The most important idea I can share is that the world is changing, the vibrational patterns are speeding up and leading us into a new era. This may take a long time, but it has begun. Understanding what is happening can help the transition go more smoothly because there will be bumps along the way. The old "ways" will fight it. They don't want change, and they will use fear as their main weapon. You can see this everyday on the news. Fear of everything. The opposite of love is fear, not hate. Fear stops love, stops higher energy from coming through. Fear is truly the enemy, and it will be used as a weapon. Man will turn against man in fear because some will believe what they've been told, that "those" people (name any religion, race, gender, or lifestyle you wish) are out to harm us in some way. In reality "those" people are the same as us! We are all souls on Earth for this time period, they are not different. Language, skin and hair color, beliefs and ways of life do not make us different. We are all souls! We simply cannot allow fear to stop love of our fellow man.

Imagine what your life would be like without television, newspapers, and social media, and if you had to live by what you witness yourself with your own eyes. Think of your life as it is right now; is it full of danger and fear? Not from the news, but from your own interactions with real people around you. Maybe that is where we should spend more of our energy and attention. Ninety-nine percent of what I see on the news doesn't affect me directly. Sure, sometimes there is information about health insurance or the weather that is important to me, but wouldn't I find those things out anyway? The insurance companies send me information all the time in the mail about how much "protection" and more importantly, "coverage" I need. Should I be worried? It is what it is, and the media lives off of revenue created by advertising. The price for advertising time is dependent upon ratings. The higher the ratings, the more they can change their clients. News ratings are fickle, but the more sensational and dangerous things are it seems the more people will tune in. Fear is the key ingredient to news success. And outrage. Keep the folks keyed up, scared, worried, and nervous and the more they will watch. Ka-ching! It is a business, but unfortunately it thrives on fear and danger.

Step Up!

Please do not hesitate to join the awakening souls throughout the world whose goal is to spread love rather than fear, and to share their understanding of what is happening. It starts within you and moves out from there. Imagine if everyone felt this way and lived their path fully! This can happen, and I believe it will happen.

Interviews and Questions

Waking up to Spirit is my theme here, as it was in my first book, and it is the idea that resonates with me so strongly that I return to it often. There are many souls waking up and beginning the process of discovery at this time on the Earth and as I share what I feel there may be some questions still not answered. I am learning as we all are and it is a fun, wonderful journey. I thought I would try something a little different to end this book. This next part of the book is twofold: in the first part I will "interview" myself with the questions I've had over the last few years, and then provide the best answers I can. In the second part, I will ask my Spiritual guides to comment directly!

I Interview Myself

Q: How did this start, how did you know that there was a Spiritual world that you should explore?

A: I felt something was missing in my life since I was a child, that I had somehow not found the true meaning for being here, and no one seemed to be talking about it. I suspect everyone feels this at times. Something inside me kept telling me that I should keep asking questions and searching and someday meaning would appear. It really picked up around age twenty, but was pretty dormant until just a few years ago. When I discovered there were "others" who had the same interest and met to discuss it regularly, I found acceptance and guidance. It felt like a big step in the right direction!

Q: Do we need to tell people about our awakening, in other words, can we explore this new reality and knowledge without opening up about it to our family and friends?

A: Of course! The only ones I've discussed this with really are my wife and a little with my grown children. I don't bring it up to others unless they show an interest or hint of their own awakening. Remember, this is new to lots of people, it goes against much of our traditional church teachings, so study on your own and you will find others that are also interested. I have close friends who don't know I've published books and have a Spiritual-themed website. You learn to gauge others' interests along the way.

Q: Why do you feel you should write these books? What do you get out of it?

A: I get plenty out of it. Lots of ideas and clarification for my own life during the process of writing. My guides seem to know what I need to find out and learn, and they certainly move me in certain directions and to topics that seem useful. I keep a journal that helps me a great deal, and often I go there to ask my guides questions when I'm not sure of something, Spiritual or not. Somehow a balance comes to me and I can move on. If I never sold a book ever I would still feel wonderful and enriched by the process I've gone through. Money is not a factor in this, the information is. If the sales of books can pay for itself and the publisher and I don't have debts afterward, I am happy.

I felt the need to write these books and get them out there from some inner desire to share with others who are awakening at this time like I am. I have had enough positive feedback to convince me I am on the right path, and if someone's fears are lessened by reading this material I am more than repaid for the effort.

Q: Who are your Spirit Guides, do they have names, do you see them? And how did you connect with them in the first place?

A: Great questions! You might add, how do I know they are real? Well, that is the step that took me a while. As I mentioned, I kept a journal about all things Spiritual in my life and it seemed that ideas came quickly and easily, and the amount I wrote was amazing to me. I usually had to go back and read what I had written to see if it made sense. You see, the words would form in my mind as I typed, not so much as sentences, but as phrases or even single words, so I didn't usually know where a thought was going until it was complete. This was strange, but it did occur to me that I was getting ideas from outside myself, or from an inner part of myself that I was not aware of. The more I thought about it, and researched, the more I grew in confidence that this input was being given to me for some reason.

As far as names are concerned, well, I don't know that part exactly. I know some psychic folks absolutely do know their guides' names. I haven't really asked, I guess. The way I picture my guides is like this: I think I have one master guide who stays with me and oversees the input I get and the communications between myself and the Spirit world. I picture "him" as a male, but it doesn't mean anything. I also see a sort of revolving group of souls around him who come and go, who help when they are needed. He always has input from them. I feel like my guides and I are a team, and when I pass from this physical life I will be reunited with this "family" of souls and will know them all, even better than those I know on Earth. As we incarnate we work with a group of souls and will understand all of this when we leave the physical realm. There is nothing but love between the souls, and our guides want only good for us.

Q: Do Spirit Guides of others work together? In other words, do your guides work with someone else's guides?

A: Yes! Guides can call in information and help and suggestions from other guides whenever they wish, after all, they don't sleep... But seriously, as we incarnate to Earth we stay in contact with our guides at a higher level than our usual physical selves can detect. This part of communication is mostly hidden or lost to us—unless we meditate, and start to awaken in a Spiritual sense. This helps us to open the channels and as with most skills, the more we practice, the better we get. We can request our guides work with a particular person's to help us or that person as needed. I find the image I have and feeling I get from my guides is one of pure love, and humor! I do things that I start laughing at and feel like

I'm sharing with them. It is a wonderful feeling to connect with your guides, and even though you don't realize it, you are connecting all the time. You'll have a thought about doing something or going somewhere and you may wonder why that popped into your head. Well, it may have been placed there, but your free will allows you to do whatever you wish. Sometimes I suddenly want to go for a drive in the country. Hmmm, where did that come from? And as I do I notice the changing of the leaves or the wispy clouds, or maybe I see some wildlife, and any of these can change my mood in a positive way.

Q: But what about demons and evil spirits? Could they tap into what you were doing?

A: I have always gone on "gut" instincts and feelings. They have never let me down that I can recall. The impressions and words that came through me always have a positive feel to them. There is positive energy involved and I never have had any fear or worry. Are there evil spirits, etc.? I don't know. I haven't felt any or experienced anything of the sort, so I hope not. Seems the "evil" in the world is more the result of fear. Maybe we create demons and so on within ourselves through fear. Hopefully we won't have to find out! I stay as positive as I can at all times and trust my guides to take me in the right direction. They have never let me down or caused me to doubt. There are many who talk about evil spirits, but I think that we create our own.

Q: Do you keep the Spiritual feeling and focus all the time?

A: Not at all, though I try to keep it close. There are many times when I am simply existing, doing what we all do without a thought of any of this. And that is perfectly OK, nothing needs to be in our mind all the time. However, as I've learned to accept (remember—awareness is first, then acceptance), the spiritual feeling seems to be a part of me, in the background, but there. When I find myself in a situation, the Spiritual side almost always pops up to help me with my decisions. If someone says something that makes me upset the thought that they are a kindred soul on their own Spiritual journey helps change my reaction and keeps me away from confrontation and arguing. This can happen throughout the day, and smooth out the ups and downs.

Q: Speaking of ups and downs, how do you deal with them in your newly awakening state?

A: They will still come in all areas; Spirituality, physical health, emotional balance, and so on, so I deal with them the same as anyone else, but as I said in the last question, my Spiritual side will often have more energy and allow me to see things in a better way. Sometimes I really do feel low, as we all do, and I will ask my guides for help. Remember, you can always ask for help, you don't have to know who your guides are, or really anything about them to ask. Just ask. Give them permission to help you with a situation you have, to suggest the best answers and responses. They want to help, but cannot interfere. You must give them permission. Don't expect miracles all the time, though that is a possibility! Your guides will not go against your free will or your chosen Spiritual path, but if you're at the mall and really need a parking space, ask them for it and it will probably show up! This always surprises me, but it is true.

Ups and downs, well the ups are pretty easy to deal with, the downs have built-in help—your Spirit Guides! Keep in mind that we are humans, and we will go through many emotional and physical trying times, those are part of our incarnation to experience. Embrace them and ask your guides to help you understand why these are happening and what you should learn from them.

Q: Is there a way to be less judgmental? I often see behavior that I feel is inappropriate, or the way someone looks isn't right, and then realize I am judging them. This seems difficult to eliminate, don't you think?

A: Sure is! We've been raised in this society to look at and evaluate most everything we see and experience, including people! This is a challenge, but as we become aware of what we are doing we can "catch" ourselves and dismiss the judgmental thoughts. When we feel balanced, we no longer need to boost our self-esteem with comparisons. As always, awareness leads to acceptance, both of others and ourselves. We are humans with lots of flaws, and learning to stop self-judgment is a step in the right direction, though for some it is a real challenge. We've all known people who are constantly down on themselves. If only they would stop criticizing themselves! As we awaken, we filter our thoughts through a more positive element, love—the strongest filter in the world.

Q: How can I tell if a Spiritual person like a medium or card reader is genuine? Aren't there some that are in it for other reasons, like money or attention?

A: Sure, as in any business or way of life, there are those who are real and those who are maybe less so. I've seen them myself. Often one discovers they have an ability and they wish to share it, but humans are somewhat complex and the ego is always wanting something. This can lead to a change in motivation, possibly from helping others to making money. This isn't necessarily wrong, money is needed, but the drive can change. Can one use their talents and still make a living? Yes! But be aware of the temptations of the material world, they can throw you off the tracks, so to speak.

As for telling how "genuine" a person is, that is a case of feeling it in your gut. I go into a meeting of this kind feeling positive and believing, and then my heart will tell me how well they connect with me. It is sad that there are those out just to make a buck using their abilities, or pretending they even have abilities, but it is part of the landscape of humanity. Trust your gut, you will know. I happen to believe that many, if not most, are wonderful, loving, sharing people. But sometimes ... remember, we are all human and make mistakes.

Q: How can I find a Spiritual or psychic or mystical kind of discussion group to join? Do they cost money?

A: If you are in a larger town or city you will probably find them easily. In rural areas, I'm not so sure. Do an Internet search for something like "Spirituality Groups in (put your town's name here)." Here, where I live in Omaha, Nebraska, quite a few popped up. A good way to find them is by visiting www.meetup.com and searching for "Spirituality." Don't hesitate to ask like-minded friends and acquaintances if they know of any such groups. Those that I've attended were filled with positive energy and very helpful. As I mentioned earlier in the book, you will have to go by the feeling you get from a group to decide to return or not. Sometimes the meetings or content is simply not for you. Look around, there will be others. Or you can do what we did at my house, we simply started our own. We asked a few folks who were genuinely interested to come over for talks on our deck or in the dining area. Very informal, and very useful. Soon we had others asking to attend! Rarely have I seen a group that charged money for attending, almost all are free. However, sometimes a room has to be reserved and has a fee, and in that case please pony up your share.

Q: I am afraid others in my family won't like this or understand what I am feeling. How do I deal with them?

A: This is a situation that often comes up. As I felt myself awakening I simply kept it to myself, didn't discuss it much with friends or coworkers. I knew many of them would be skeptical or wouldn't understand. I guess the best way is to always look within yourself for answers. Is there a need to explain your new interests? No, not really, unless they notice something and want to talk about it, or ask questions. Remember, actions speak louder than words. Live your new knowledge, let your guides help you, and you will know best how to deal with family and friends. You may be surprised how many of them are actually interested or would become interested. Be sincere, don't sugarcoat, don't overexplain, don't overact what you are waking up to. Be yourself and remember that we are all together in this journey and can support each other regardless of where we are on our paths.

I know of some friends who feel their families will disown them for believing in such nonsense! It bothers them, but life goes on. Some people have closed their minds to the world of Spirit and some have not. Allow them their own choice, no need to convert! If you find a discussion group you may react like I did, "This is great, others who want to talk about this stuff!" It is also possible the group may turn you off completely, as in any human interaction. But don't hesitate to give it a try if you feel the calling.

Q: Can this Spiritual approach work with organized religions? I belong to a church and would like to continue going.

A: Your approach to the Universe is unique to you, and you have the power and right to find the balance that works. Churches can have very positive effects on attendees, and a group that worships together can raise their own Spiritual vibrations. It is a matter of intent. Do you go to church simply because you always have gone? Is it a mere habit? Do you get a good feeling from attendance? Or do you go because you feel you have to? Unfortunately, I've seen fear used too many times to keep folks in line. (Fire and brimstone!) This gets into the whole discussion of Heaven and Hell, which would be more suited to another time or book.

Some religions are very Spiritual in nature and some are not so much. As with most things on Earth, you must decide your path.

Message from My Guides

Q: To my wonderful guides, do you have anything you would like to add to this narrative directly? Thank you for your input throughout this process and throughout my life!

A: We are enjoying the process as you call it, and will continue to cooperate and work with you in this incarnation. There is still more work to be done, not only with you, personally, but with the world. Yes, there are huge changes afoot, and we will do our best to help those in the physical world understand and make their way through them.

There is freedom in understanding, and a clear view can be of great assistance in reaching your path's goals. We can offer hints and guidance, and will do so if you ask. Books of this kind can help that process. We have great hopes for the future of mankind, but the challenges at this time are real. Continue to go within to find who you really are.

Though there is much sadness in the world and many are frustrated and suffering, the good news is that one day they will join with all of us at the next level in happiness and joy! No one will be left behind. What is happening in their lives must happen, and their souls realize this. This does not mean they give in and give up. The struggle to rise above will continue.

Finally, let us tell you that the world can be full of joy and happiness. You decide how you want it to affect you. You have the power to control your own destiny, and attitude is where you start. Waking up each day and telling yourself that "I choose happiness today!" will start the energy moving in the best possible way.

Always remember, even in the darkest of times, that you are on Earth for a short time and then will return to your true home with those you love. Nothing ends! Life goes on, so live your physical incarnation to the fullest! Your own Spirit Guides will help you if you just ask.

To my guides:
Thank you for your input!

Acknowledgments

Kathie Bird, my wife and partner. Her encouragement makes all the difference.

Declan "Iddow Feddow" Milleson, who makes me happy every time I see him.

Murphy Sadler, whose smile lights up a room.

Stephen Bird, author extraordinaire, and my big brother.

Susan Carpenter, a true angel on Earth, my sister, whom I owe so much to.

Joyce McArthur-Johnson, my friend and sounding board, as I am hers.

Peggy Wilmes, my quiet friend whom I see far too infrequently.

Eileen Heller, always a positive bright spot whenever I see her.

Teresa Paulson, who provides me with support and confidence. She is gifted and doesn't realize it.

Carly Milleson, Nick Bird, Molly Sadler, and Tom Bird, my children.

Julia Cannon, Nancy Vernon, Brandy McDonald, and the team at Ozark Mountain Publishing who keep the word alive and are so supportive.

Adnan Ademovic, video production for UFOHub.net and Ozark Mountain Publishing.

Debbie Upton, my editor. She's a proofreading hero who doesn't miss a thing and I'm very grateful!

Ted Snow, sound editor for the audio book form.

There are many others who have contributed to this book and my life and I thank you all. The challenge of keeping a balance in this day and age pushes us to depend on each other, which makes us stronger. On we go!

About the Author

Dr. Dan Bird has been interested in Spiritual topics since he was a teenager. Though raised loosely in a religious community and even attending a parochial school from grades three through twelve, he had questions that were not satisfactorily answered within the views of the church. After many years as a musician he became a teacher and technology trainer for Nebraska's largest school district. He earned a doctorate in education from the University of Nebraska, with a focus on the use of technology in the schools. This book is the follow-up to *Waking Up in the Spiritual Age*, also published by Ozark Mountain Publishing.

A prolific songwriter, Dr. Bird has performed over fifty of his own compositions solo, in duets, trios, and even full rock and country bands. His music can be heard at http://danbirdmusic.com.

Married with four grown children, he keeps very busy traveling, writing, and adding to his Spiritual webpage: http://wakinguptospirit.com.

He lives with his wife, Kathie, in Omaha, Nebraska.

Books by Dr. Daniel Bird

Finding Your Way in the Spiritual Age
Published by: Ozark Mountain Publishing

Waking Up in the Spiritual Age
Published by: Ozark Mountain Publishing

For more information about any of the above titles, soon to be released titles,
or other items in our catalog, write, phone or visit our website:
Ozark Mountain Publishing, Inc.
PO Box 754, Huntsville, AR 72740
479-738-2348/800-935-0045
www.ozarkmt.com

Other Books by Ozark Mountain Publishing, Inc.

Dolores Cannon
A Soul Remembers Hiroshima
Between Death and Life
Conversations with Nostradamus,
    Volume I, II, III
The Convoluted Universe -Book One,
    Two, Three, Four, Five
The Custodians
Five Lives Remembered
Jesus and the Essenes
Keepers of the Garden
Legacy from the Stars
The Legend of Starcrash
The Search for Hidden Sacred Knowledge
They Walked with Jesus
The Three Waves of Volunteers and the
    New Earth
Aron Abrahamsen
Holiday in Heaven
Out of the Archives – Earth Changes
Justine Alessi & M. E. McMillan
Rebirth of the Oracle
Kathryn/Patrick Andries
Naked in Public
Kathryn Andries
The Big Desire
Dream Doctor
Soul Choices: Six Paths to Find Your Life
    Purpose
Soul Choices: Six Paths to Fulfilling
    Relationships
Patrick Andries
Owners Manual for the Mind
Dan Bird
Finding Your Way in the Spiritual Age
Waking Up in the Spiritual Age
Julia Cannon
Soul Speak – The Language of Your Body
Ronald Chapman
Seeing True
Albert Cheung
The Emperor's Stargate
Jack Churchward
Lifting the Veil on the Lost Continent of
    Mu
The Stone Tablets of Mu
Sherri Cortland
Guide Group Fridays

Raising Our Vibrations for the New Age
Spiritual Tool Box
Windows of Opportunity
Cinnamon Crow
Chakra Zodiac Healing Oracle
Teen Oracle
Patrick De Haan
The Alien Handbook
Paulinne Delcour-Min
Spiritual Gold
Michael Dennis
Morning Coffee with God
God's Many Mansions
Arun & Sunanda Gandhi
The Forgotten Woman
Carolyn Greer Daly
Opening to Fullness of Spirit
Anita Holmes
Twidders
Victoria Hunt
Kiss the Wind
Diane Lewis
From Psychic to Soul
Donna Lynn
From Fear to Love
Maureen McGill
Baby It's You
Maureen McGill & Nola Davis
Live from the Other Side
Curt Melliger
Heaven Here on Earth
Henry Michaelson
And Jesus Said – A Conversation
Dennis Milner
Kosmos
Andy Myers
Not Your Average Angel Book
Guy Needler
Avoiding Karma
Beyond the Source – Book 1, Book 2
The Anne Dialogues
The History of God
The Origin Speaks
James Nussbaumer
And Then I Knew My Abundance
The Master of Everything
Mastering Your Own Spiritual Freedom

For more information about any of the above titles, soon to be released titles,
or other items in our catalog, write, phone or visit our website:
PO Box 754, Huntsville, AR 72740
479-738-2348/800-935-0045
www.ozarkmt.com

Other Books by Ozark Mountain Publishing, Inc.

Sherry O'Brian
Peaks and Valleys
Riet Okken
The Liberating Power of Emotions
Gabrielle Orr
Akashic Records: One True Love
Let Miracles Happen
Victor Parachin
Sit a Bit
Nikki Pattillo
A Spiritual Evolution
Children of the Stars
Rev. Grant H. Pealer
A Funny Thing Happened on the
  Way to Heaven
Worlds Beyond Death
Victoria Pendragon
Born Healers
Feng Shui from the Inside, Out
Sleep Magic
The Sleeping Phoenix
Michael Perlin
Fantastic Adventures in Metaphysics
Walter Pullen
Evolution of the Spirit
Debra Rayburn
Let's Get Natural with Herbs
Charmian Redwood
A New Earth Rising
Coming Home to Lemuria
David Rivinus
Always Dreaming
Richard Rowe
Imagining the Unimaginable
M. Don Schorn
Elder Gods of Antiquity
Legacy of the Elder Gods
Gardens of the Elder Gods
Reincarnation...Stepping Stones of Life

Garnet Schulhauser
Dance of Eternal Rapture
Dance of Heavenly Bliss
Dancing Forever with Spirit
Dancing on a Stamp
Annie Stillwater Gray
Education of a Guardian Angel
The Dawn Book
Work of a Guardian Angel
Blair Styra
Don't Change the Channel
Natalie Sudman
Application of Impossible Things
L.R. Sumpter
The Old is New
We Are the Creators
Jim Thomas
Tales from the Trance
Janie Wells
Embracing the Human Journey
Payment for Passage
Dennis Wheatley/ Maria Wheatley
The Essential Dowsing Guide
Maria Wheatley
Druidic Soul Star Astrology
Jacquelyn Wiersma
The Zodiac Recipe
Sherry Wilde
The Forgotten Promise
Lyn Willmoth
A Small Book of Comfort
Stuart Wilson & Joanna Prentis
Atlantis and the New Consciousness
Beyond Limitations
The Essenes -Children of the Light
The Magdalene Version
Power of the Magdalene
Robert Winterhalter
The Healing Christ

For more information about any of the above titles, soon to be released titles,
or other items in our catalog, write, phone or visit our website:
PO Box 754, Huntsville, AR 72740
479-738-2348/800-935-0045
www.ozarkmt.com